Through the
Eyes of Children

THE FREE PRESS

Through the Eyes of Children

HEALING STORIES FOR CHILDREN OF DIVORCE

Janet R. Johnston, Ph.D.

Karen Breunig, R.N., M.S.

Carla Garrity, Ph.D.

Mitchell A. Baris, Ph.D.

Illustrated by Karen Breunig

THE FREE PRESS
A Division of Simon & Schuster Inc.
1230 Avenue of the Americas
New York, NY 10020

THE FREE PRESS and colophon are trademarks
of Simon & Schuster Inc.

Designed by Carla Bolte

Manufactured in the United States of America

10 9 8 7 6 5 4 3

Library of Congress Cataloging-in-Publication Data

Through the eyes of children: healing stories for children of divorce
    / Janet R. Johnston . . . [et al.] ; illustrated by Karen Breunig.
        p.   cm.
    Includes bibliographical references.
    ISBN 0-684-83703-X (alk. paper)
    1. Children of divorced parents—Psychology.   2. Children's
stories.   I. Johnston, Janet R.
HQ777.5.T498   1997
306.874—dc21   97-9284
                                                        CIP

ISBN 0–684–83703–X

*This book is dedicated to
the children who have taught us what we know.*

Contents

Acknowledgments

Carla thanks Chuck, Nancy, and Carol, whose wisdom and talents wove into the fabric of her family, allowing Megan and Amy to write their own stories.

Karen expresses heartfelt gratitude to those guides and teachers who have blessed her life. To her family—Peter, Simone, Lissa, Becca, and Paul. To Stephen White, Denny Webster, and Carol Montgomery. To her coauthors and friends. And, of course, to Smiley.

Introduction

Children typically suffer pain, confusion, and insecurity when their parents separate. They are especially hurt by the outbursts of anger, bitterness, lack of respect, inability to communicate, and overt hostility that can repeatedly flare up between battling parents. Despite all the obvious signs that their parents' relationship has irretrievably broken apart, most children secretly harbor, sometimes for years, fantasies that their parents might some day reconcile. At the very least, they wish their parents could be friends.

Family members, counselors, teachers, and other caretakers are profoundly concerned about how best to respond to children's pain, how to communicate with them, and how to help heal their emotional hurt, especially in the more difficult, high-conflict family situations. This small volume contains stories to help children understand and cope with parental separation and the fallout from their parents' conflict with each other. It describes how therapists, parents, and anyone else who cares can construct special stories tailored for each child's individual needs and fears. In doing this, it is important to understand the family experience from the children's point of view and to address and attempt to experience with them their deepest concerns. Some of these stories are written with younger or older children in mind. However, the theme of the story is the more important determinant of its usefulness to a child. Any of these stories could be used creatively as core themes or ideas for you and the child to elaborate your own story. Many children enjoy continuing the stories in their own voice, changing the details, adding artwork, or having a copy of their own to read as they wish.

CHILDREN'S CORE CONCERNS

Children very much want to believe their parents once loved each other and that they were born out of love and hope and good expectations for a happy family. They do not want to think that their entry into the world was an unhappy mistake or a devastating accident. Many children whose parents have never lived together or separated very soon after they were born have no memory of the good times when their parents were loving, kind, and generous with each other. It is sad to see how many of these children in their growing-up years will cling to any evidence of a once happy family unit, sometimes imagining it from an offhand remark or seeing it in a salvaged photograph of their parents in bygone days, together and smiling. If they are ever to be able to accept the finality of their parents' divorce, children need to understand, in an age-appropriate way, why their parents' marriage broke up. Just as adults need to have their own accounting as to why the marriage failed, so do their children need a clear explanation for the reasons their parents cannot live together.

When the divorce is an especially difficult one, with entrenched conflict, distrust, and bitterness that continues for years afterward, the children have a special set of concerns:

First, depending on their age and level of understanding, children struggle with the puzzle of their parents' conflicting claims and counter-allegations about each other (which are true and which are not?). Children often witness only a part of a parental dispute or overhear only half of a telephone conversation and can be very confused about what is really happening (who did what to whom?). Some of the possibilities, from a child's very literal viewpoint, seem truly frightening. For example, six-year-old Bobbie pondered anxiously, "Did Daddy *throw* Mommy out of the house, or did another man *steal* Mommy from Daddy?" Five-year-old Karen asked, "Is Daddy's new girlfriend really a *witch?*" The ability of children to interpret real-life events is limited; they are often afraid to seek explanations for what is happening, based on the scary clues they perceive. Ordinarily, children use their parents as a social reference for what is safe and trustworthy. Children in difficult divorce situations, however, have the profound dilemma of making sense out of vastly contradictory views communicated by the hostility, fear, and distrust between their opposing parents. In the confusion that surrounds divorce, they are left to try and figure out for themselves who is safe, who is dangerous, and who can be trusted.

Second, because of the often profound emotional neediness of their distressed parents, these children become
urgently concerned about the emotional and physical
well-being of a parent. For example, they often wonder,
"Will Mommy be sad and cry if she is on her own while
we go visit Daddy?" These worries about the well-being of
a parent are often fused with nagging fears about their own
vulnerability to being abandoned, lost, ignored, or even
destroyed in the parental fights, which for them are very
frightening ("If I visit my daddy, will my mommy be there
when I get back? Will she be mad at me?"). Consequently,
these children are often highly attuned to the task of taking
care of a parent's feelings, and they tend to constrict or
hide their own needs and feelings.

Third, because they are often the centerpiece of their
parents' arguments with each other, to varying degrees,
these children feel responsible for causing the disputes,
yet most feel helpless to control or stop the conflict.
While the younger children tend to believe that something they did caused the fight, the older ones believe the
fights occur simply because they exist: "If I were dead,
they wouldn't need to fight anymore," nine-year-old
Tracy told her counselor. Exciting feelings of great power
and self-importance are juxtaposed with a frightening
sense of their smallness and overwhelming inadequacy in
the face of their parents' intractable anger. Faced with this
paradox, the child's developing sense of being competent,
self-determined, and appropriately empowered in the
world is threatened. These children often have trouble as-
serting their own needs and wishes. It is easier for them

to remain compliant and try to please others; that is, until their own neediness overwhelms them.

Fourth, in those situations where parents continually put each other down, children are clearly concerned with the problem of who is good and who is bad, and with whom they should identify. At the same time, they are instinctively aware that they are the product of both parents. Four-year-old Andy revealed his predicament when, over and over again, he played out a scene in which a boy doll was in the center of a battlefield; as he put it, "the good people wore bad masks and the bad people wore good masks." Children become confused, ashamed, and self-accusing if they feel they have become like the "bad" parent. In this spotlighting of parental faults and failures, important developmental tasks are made more difficult; it is very difficult for these children to accept and integrate "bad" with "good" into a more realistic view of each parent and, at the same time, form a cohesive sense of themselves in which they can tolerate their own imperfections.

Fifth, children have a very limited store of coping strategies when faced with these dilemmas. Unfortunately, distressed parents are not always able to distinguish their own feelings and concerns from those of their children. Nor are parents in emotional turmoil always good role models for how to handle upsetting feelings and conflict in a constructive, moral way. Children also find it difficult to talk about sensitive topics and feelings with either of their disputing parents because they fear they might escalate the fight or get caught in the middle. Instead, some turn inward, trying to make do with their own meager resources.

Consequently, they end up feeling depressed and inadequate when their efforts to cope are not successful.

In working with children struggling to come to terms with their parents' separation and living apart, we have found that the use of special imaginative stories, which reflect their particular family situations and central concerns, can provide an effective way to help children understand what is happening in their families, and at the same time allow them to express expectable feelings and show them different ways of coping. These stories can provide a brief intervention for children coping with normal developmental concerns, or they can be woven into the individual or group therapy for more distressed children, particularly those from highly conflicted and violent family situations.

HOW TO CONSTRUCT A CHILD'S STORY OF PARENTAL SEPARATION

Children may be helped by stories about their parents' relationship that include the following elements:

1. The narrative should provide a positive blueprint, a story or family-life tale in which there are no villains or heroes—just essentially humane characters (whether animals or people) who are well intentioned but who nevertheless make mistakes and have very human vulnerabilities as well as strengths.

2. The story should positively and realistically portray the parents' good intentions—how they loved each other in the

beginning and had very positive ideals and goals in getting together, marrying, and having children. It should describe the parents' special qualities and note that these are what attracted each parent to the other in the first place. (This is well illustrated in several of the stories, including "Hector Horse," "The Lions of Africa," and "Robbie Rabbit.")

3. The story should explain concretely how the parents were not able to satisfy each other in some important ways and how, for these reasons, the parents were disappointed, frustrated, and made each other unhappy. It is important not only to demonstrate the irreconcilable nature of the parents' differences but also to comment on how they tried and failed to make their relationship work. Negative personal attributes can be reframed in nonjudgmental ways as value differences between parents (as in "The Turtle Story," in which a land turtle marries a sea turtle); or they can be reframed as special, albeit troublesome capacities in the basic, enduring nature of a parent (such as the explosive volcano in the "Elephant Island" story, or the need of the circus performer to take dangerous risks in the "Spunky" story).

4. The story should name the child's expectable feelings and dilemmas as a consequence of the parents' divorce and disputes with each other. It might address an anxiety about protecting and nurturing a distressed parent (as in the "Claudio and Petra" story) or managing the drug and alcohol dependence of a parent (as in the "Spunky" story). It might involve trying to decide who is right and who is wrong, and who is good and who is bad

(as in the "Hector Horse" story); how to assert one's own feelings, needs, and ideas without getting caught in the middle of the parental conflict (as in the story "The Giraffe Who Couldn't Speak"); or the need to acknowledge anger about the parents' divorce and reconciliation fantasies (as in the "Robbie Rabbit" story).

5. The story can explain how the child is trying to cope with confusing dilemmas and then show how the problem can be thought about in new ways. Specifically, it can suggest new coping strategies and new moral rules that can guide the child's responses to the family dilemmas (as in all the stories).

6. Most important, the story should include clearly shown and stated permission for the child to have a continuing relationship with each parent and to love both of them. It will be most helpful if it can show how the child can select good parts of each parent to identify with and how to weave those good parts into a cohesive self that is good, competent, and lovable (see especially "The Turtle Story," "The Dancers," "Hector Horse," and "The Lions of Africa").

HOW TO INCORPORATE THE PSYCHOLOGICAL ELEMENTS OF HEALING

Ideally, a healing story both engages the child and imparts a means for coping with the difficult divorce situation. An array of psychological coping strategies can be drawn on and interwoven into the story. The healing message is most likely to be incorporated by the child if it is realistic and appropriate to the unique circumstances of the child's divorce experience, is delivered within the metaphor of the story, and is within the repertoire of the child to adopt. The following guidelines can be used in selecting one or more coping techniques:

1. Humor. Children adore humor, as it entertains, gives permission to release feelings and tension, and conveys a less serious tone to an often frightening or overwhelming situation.

2. Identification. Finding a friend during a time of crisis can be extraordinarily healing. Studies from children who cope well and who are resilient indicate that they frequently master difficult situations when they have a special someone who cares about them. A story can build in that someone, such as "Smiley" in "Elephant Island," who guides the children to caves for refuge and to the waterfall for fun. Spunky finds a friend in Juneau, who offers nurturance and understanding during the most difficult moments. A story can offer just one friend or a reference group or peer group, as "The Lions of Africa" does for a young adolescent ready for the early steps toward emancipation.

3. Mirroring. Knowing and understanding someone else who has been through a similar situation and coped can be healing as well. The message that "you are not alone" imparts understanding, empathy, and hope for the future. Seeing someone else work through a similar, or the very same, set of circumstances in a satisfactory way is richly rewarding. Children will take note of the coping

means the character uses and frequently will incorporate this coping into their own behavior strategies.

4. Helping others. Sharing of oneself to help others is a valuable coping strategy for trauma, especially in older children. The story of "Spunky" demonstrates this technique when Spunky, who longs for more nurturance from his daredevil mother, feeds and plays with the seal. By taking care of the seal, Spunky also nurtures himself and not only feels better but gains awareness and insight into his own pain and loneliness.

5. Wise person. A wise character built into the story can nurture a child's growing capacity to choose good mentors to guide his or her decisions. It can also impart the coping strategies unique to what is the most problematic for an individual child. For example, a wise person might guide a child toward solutions as the giraffe story does by incorporating an animal doctor who dispenses a wonderful prescription for coping with two conflicting value systems. The child is instructed not to attempt to integrate but rather to cope by building disengagement between two parental figures and building a relationship with each one individually. This is often the only adaptive solution for a child caught in a very high-conflict divorce situation. Smiley is also a wise person in the "Elephant Island" story when he imparts wisdom about coping with a volatile parent.

It is critical that the coping strategy conveyed through the story be realistic. Holding out hope for something that will not be obtainable or is too mature for a child's developmental level will probably not be perceived by the child as healing or as helpful. Notice that in the "Spunky" story, Juneau does not impart the message that he can rescue Spunky from the circus or from the whirlwind life he must live as part of the circus, but he does offer solace and comfort during the difficult moments, and he also defines a sense of hope for the future. Juneau allows Spunky to know that there is a life outside the circus that may someday be Spunky's life as well. Juneau is a friend who will always be there even if he is no longer part of Spunky's daily life. To have Juneau take Spunky with him when he leaves the circus would have imparted an unrealistic message to a child who is not free to opt to change his or her circumstances. The technique is one of offering realistic means for coping with the present as well as hope for the future. When children are offered some resources to draw on, they often model them through understanding the healing message of the story, and they will adopt these means as their own.

Many children find that talking openly about their family situation is extremely difficult because it makes them frightened, anxious, sad, or even ashamed. Stories are an indirect way of communicating to children, allowing them to distance themselves enough to think and feel things that they might otherwise try to repress or avoid. For this reason each story needs to be a combination of the concrete and the fanciful. Like a fable, it should be sufficiently disguised from reality so that the child can tolerate what is being said without becoming too defensive. It should also be sensitive to the child's level of understanding in the complexity of information it portrays and with the coping skills it suggests. (Note that the "Elephant Island" and "Spunky" stories are appropriately veiled in symbolism for older or more defensive children.)

It is our experience that in talking with children, it is not necessary to make explicit comparisons between their situation and the characters in the story. Children tend to choose what makes sense to them and ignore what does not fit with their concerns, and they should be allowed these choices. In general, it is important to let children initiate any comment or discussion as to how much they feel either the same as or different from their counterpart in the fable.

Finally, to be of the most benefit to children within the context of their particular family, the story must be constructed with both parents' ideas and feelings in mind. The story needs to acknowledge what each can provide for the child and give permission for the child to love and identify with them both.

Writing a healing story within the metaphor is easier for some than for others. The author must start with a knowledge of the child's world image, be very empathic with the child's particular situation, and understand the issues that are painful for the child to acknowledge openly. Incorporating animals into the story is an easy tool for portraying special characteristics and temperaments. Activities in which a child takes pleasure can be built into the metaphor, such as the waterfall in "Elephant Island" for a girl who excelled at swimming and gymnastics. The child's therapist is an ideal person for writing or contributing to writing such a story and then integrating it into the therapeutic work. A creative guardian ad litem, parent coordinator, or school counselor might also try to participate in constructing such a story. A children's divorce group could be a wonderful avenue for the sharing of stories. Ideally, the individual story becomes the child's to take home, to read over and over again, and to share with both parents. In the best of all possible worlds, parents themselves might try working together on a story for their child. This would require them to collaborate on a symbolic story about their courtship, marriage, and separation, and their common love for their child. Sadly, many high-conflict parents, who have children who most need these stories, are unlikely to be able to work together. Sometimes reading a story that has been written by someone else might provide parents with greater compassion and empathy for their child and thereby facilitate healing for the parents as well.

PART I

Common Divorce Concerns

CHAPTER 1

The Turtle Story

JANET JOHNSTON

It is difficult for many children to understand why their parents are not able to live together. For some children of divorce, the parents may not even be able to communicate together, make joint decisions, or be face-to-face at any time. This story of a sand turtle and a sea turtle presents a simple, clear, and non-judgmental explanation of parents who cannot cooperate. At the same time, it acknowledges and supports a child's need to be free to love both mother and father and to be accepted as having traits similar to each parent.

Once upon a time, there was a sand turtle named Sammy. Sammy lived in the sand by the ocean, just near the edge of the woods. Every day he loved to lie in the sun on the sandy beach. He also liked to make tunnels and secret hideaways in the sand dunes. His favorite food was sand crabs. Nearby in the ocean there was a sea turtle whose name was Sally. Sally lived deep in the ocean and loved to frolic and swim in the waves. She loved to feel the cool blue-green water on her body as she hunted for jellyfish to eat.

One day Sammy the sand turtle crawled to the water's edge to look for sand crabs. At the same time, Sally the sea turtle swam to the shallow part of the beach where she could poke her head out of the water to see the blue sky. All at once Sally and Sammy's eyes met and they fell in love. Sally had never seen a sand turtle before, and she thought he looked different and handsome in his dark brown shell. Sammy had never seen a sea turtle before, and he thought Sally's blue-green shell was so different and just the prettiest he had ever seen.

The two turtles loved each other so much that they decided to get married. For a time they lived at the water's edge so that Sammy could sit on the sand and keep dry and warm while Sally sat in the shallow water to keep cool. Pretty soon they had two baby turtles, named Tommy and Tina. These little baby turtles had very nice brown and blue-green shells. They looked something like each of their parents.

Tommy and Tina Turtle loved to play in the sand with their father, Sammy. They would spend hours digging tunnels and searching for sand crabs to eat. Sometimes they would take naps side by side in the warm sand. When they pulled in their heads and legs, their shells looked like rocks sticking halfway out of the sand. Tommy and Tina also loved to frolic in the sea with their mother, Sally.

They did somersaults in the waves and explored the underwater caves and reefs, looking for jellyfish for dinner. For a while this was a happy family of turtles.

But then something went wrong! Tommy and Tina Turtle were having so much fun that they didn't notice that Sammy, the father sand turtle, was spending less and less time at the water's edge. He wandered up into the sand dunes and hunted for food in the woods. Sally, the mother sea turtle, spent all her time swimming in the deep part of the ocean, and she did not sit in the shallow water on the beach anymore. Each night, when the father and mother turtles met to feed the kid turtles some dinner, they would argue and fight. Sometimes Sammy the sand turtle and Sally the sea turtle snapped at each other. Tommy and Tina were scared they might hurt each other. Sometimes the mother and father turtles refused to talk to each other. Sammy, the father sand turtle, would pull his head into his shell and dig into the sand, and Sally, the mother sea turtle, turned her back on him and dove into the ocean. Finally one day, Sammy and Sally decided they didn't want to live together anymore. Sally decided to live at the bottom of the ocean, and Sammy decided to live up in the sand dunes above the beach.

Tommy and Tina Turtle were very sad. They were still young turtles and needed someone to look after them. They loved both their mom and their dad and wanted to be with both of them all the time. Tommy was kind of angry, and he yelled a lot and had fights with his mom. Tina was angry, too, but she kept her feelings inside and hid in her shell all day. She wouldn't even play with her

Finally, one day, Sammy and Sally decided they didn't want to live together anymore. Sally decided to live at the bottom of the ocean, and Sammy decided to live up in the sand dunes above the beach.

brother or any of her friends. Most of all, Tommy and Tina Turtle wanted their parents to live together at the water's edge and to be a happy family again.

One day they decided to ask the Wise Old Owl to help them. The Wise Old Owl always gave good advice to all the animals, and he could fix almost any problem. Early the next morning they packed a picnic lunch and set off for the forest to look for the Wise Old Owl. He was sleeping in the tree when they arrived, but he woke up and invited them into his tree stump. Very soon they told him the problem. Tina Turtle then asked, "Can you make our mother and father live together again?" And Tommy Turtle said, "Please, please make them love each other again!"

The Wise Old Owl stared thoughtfully into the sky for some time and then he said: "A sand turtle should NEVER marry a sea turtle. They are each two different kinds of turtles. Sammy the sand turtle likes to live on the land and sit in the warm sun. Sally the sea turtle likes to live in the ocean and swim in the cool blue water. When they live together at the water's edge they are both un-happy, cross, and angry. It is much better that they live in places where they are happy again!

"But you, Tommy Turtle, and you, Tina Turtle, are each half a sand turtle and half a sea turtle. You can live in the ocean and eat jellyfish *and* you can live on the land and eat sand crabs. You can have fun with your mother and you can also have fun with your father. They love you very much and they want you to be happy. The best plan is for you to live some of the time in the water with your mother and some of the time on land with your father."

And that is just what Tommy Turtle and Tina Turtle did! Sometimes they lived in the deep blue ocean and practiced their swimming with their mother, and sometimes they lived on the warm, sunny sand and practiced hunting in the country with their father. They made lots of friends with all the fish and dolphins and whales in the ocean, and they made lots of friends with the deer and the badgers and the foxes in the woods. They loved their mother and they loved their father. In fact, Tommy and Tina became happy again and grew up to be a new kind of turtle, with beautiful brownish-bluish-green–colored shells, that could live both in the ocean and on the land.

CHAPTER 2

The Bird Family Story

KAREN BREUNIG

Financial necessity forces some families to be separated by long distances following a divorce. Maintaining a relationship at a distance is not easy for children. When the distant parent remarries and acquires a stepchild, the children may feel even more of a sense of rejection and replacement. Continuing to feel loved and cared about when one parent is living a distance away is the theme of "The Bird Family Story."

Once upon a time, long ago, high in the purple mountains that rose out of the golden plain, there lived a family of birds. They were very colorful birds, with bright orange beaks and feathers of red and yellow. The song they sang was more beautiful than any that had ever been heard in these mountains. They lived in a nest atop a tall evergreen from where they could see the mountains all around and the blue sky above. The sky where they lived was very big indeed, and the three young birds of the family were just starting to test their wings in that very big sky.

The mother bird was from a family of birds that migrate every spring and every autumn. In the spring, when the earth woke up from its winter sleep, they liked to be up in the mountains. The flowers and grasses and insects were abundant during the golden mountain summer. In the fall, they flew to wherever there was food and warm sun.

The father bird was from a family of birds that didn't particularly like to migrate. They had long ago found a comfortable nest for themselves down on the plain, at the foot of the mountains, and they had settled in. There they stayed for many years.

Soon after the father bird and the mother bird met, they decided to get married. They picked the nest high in the evergreen in which to start their family. It was safe and secure and offered a wonderful view of the plains below. They hoped Mama would be happy because she would be closer to the warm sun that she loved. They hoped Papa would be happy because he could see the golden plains that he loved.

Soon the babies started arriving. The mother bird and father bird were delighted with their babies. They brought them food and kept them warm and safe at night. They sang to them every morning and every evening. And they began to teach them to fly.

Now, about this time, the mother bird and father bird began to realize that they were really very different from each other. After all, the mother bird was from a family of birds that called many different places home. When winter came, she thought about her brothers and sisters who were far south enjoying the warm sun. This made Mama restless.

Sometimes Papa found himself gazing off in the direction of the plains from which he had come. He found himself wishing he could live there again. He liked the big wide open spaces of the plains. Sometimes the mountains felt too crowded for him. This made him restless. Mama and Papa started to feel the tension grow between them. Neither of them was happy. It became harder and harder for them to be the kind of friends that live together.

One sad day, they decided it was time for them to live in separate nests. They both loved their young birds very much. They both wanted to continue to take good care of them, and to teach them to sing and to fly. Mama loved being their mother and Papa loved begin their father. That would never change. They would always be parents together. Perhaps if they lived in separate nests, they could become a different kind of friend, friends that raise their babies together.

Papa bird moved to another nest down on the golden plains. The baby birds stayed there with their Papa part of the week. Then he would fly them back up the mountain to Mama's nest in the evergreen. They continued their singing lessons and their flying lessons. They grew bigger and started to be able to take a few short flights around the nest.

Now about this time, Mama bird started to feel the urge to move to where the food was more abundant. Up in the mountains summer was gone and winter was just over the ridge. She worried about being able to feed her young birds now that the frost lay heavy on the grass every morning. Where would she find worms and insects to feed them when the snow covered the ground?

Papa bird was able to gather food for his children down on the plains. He had grown up there and he knew where to look. But he couldn't gather enough food to feed them every day. He needed Mama bird's help. Taking care of young birds takes two parents.

Mama bird came to Papa bird and told him about her worries. She told him she was thinking about moving to where it was easier for her to take care of their children. He knew it was hard for Mama bird to gather enough food for their young when winter was upon the mountains. And Mama was not a bird of the plains. She was a migrating bird. She knew if she could just move on she would be able to find a place where she could find food for the children.

What a hard time for Mama bird and Papa bird. They both wanted to be with the baby birds. They both wanted to watch them grow up, watch them learn to sing and fly. They talked and talked and talked, trying to come up with a plan that would be best for their children. None of the plans were perfect. None of them made everybody happy.

These young birds were part like their Mama, migrating birds, and part like their Papa, birds of the golden prairie. So it was decided that they would migrate with their mother to a new place, far away, where Mama felt she could find food for them. But it was also decided that a few times during the year they would migrate back to the golden plains, to the nest where their father lived.

And Papa too would make a journey every so often to see the young birds where they lived with their Mama.

The plan proved to be very hard at times. Sometimes the young birds missed their Papa very much. Lots of times their Papa missed them very much. Sometimes it was hard for Mama bird to take care of them without Papa bird nearby to help out. But Mama was able to find food for them in their new home. And Papa helped out as much as possible, bringing what food he could whenever he visited, and sending many wonderful surprises by airmail almost every week.

The young birds continued to grow. Their flying skills were getting better and better. They became known all through the woods that they lived in for their lovely singing. As they grew older, they each began to sing a new song, different from each other. The songs were something like their Papa's song, something like their Mama's song, but mostly they were new songs, their own songs. They were proud of themselves.

They soon became old enough to migrate back to their Papa's nest by themselves. They were good flyers and were strong enough to fly all day long, even against strong winds. Their Papa was always so happy to see them. He planned lots of excursions for them when they came. He always made sure they returned for a while to the tall, beautiful evergreen on the top of the purple mountain where they had been born.

One day, when they arrived at their Papa's nest after a long journey from their Mama's home, they were very surprised to find that Papa bird had moved into a new nest.

This nest belonged to another mama bird who had a young bird of her own. Papa bird was now making this nest his own. Tessa, the youngest of Papa's birds, wondered to herself if this place would ever feel like home to her. There was a warm place for her to sleep at night. There was enough food to go around. And Papa still gave her lots of love and attention, helping her with her flying and her singing.

When it came time for the three young birds to migrate back to their Mama's nest, Tessa became restless. She came to her father and asked, "Papa, do you love this mama bird that lives here with you?" Papa answered, "Yes." "Papa," she continued, "are you going to marry this mama bird?" "Yes," Papa said. Tessa got very quiet. A tear glistened in the corner of her eye. Papa saw it and moved closer. He leaned down and looked into her eyes and said, "Tessa, my wild and wonderful little bird, what is making you so sad?" "Nothing, Papa," she said. For she herself truly didn't know.

When Tessa got back to her Mama's nest, she was not acting like herself. Mama bird asked her what was wrong, but Tessa didn't know what to say. She just knew she felt a great sadness in her heart. She flew out to her favorite part of the woods and sat quietly on the branch of a tall and stately oak. She didn't feel like singing.

Soon, her friend the squirrel, who lived in that stately oak, took notice of her and her sadness. "What is it, my friend?" he asked. "I'm not really sure, Squirrel," she said. "I just migrated back here from my father's nest. I miss him very much. Sometimes this migrating is really hard. And now my Papa is sharing a nest with another mama bird and a young bird too. Do you think Papa might grow to love them so much that he would forget about me? After all, he is with them every day, and he is with me only sometimes."

"I don't know how to answer that, little bird. But I think I know someone who can help. You wait right here." With that, Squirrel scurried down the huge trunk and off in the direction of the creek. Soon he returned followed closely by a tall, graceful bear covered with silver fur. "Dear little bird," said the squirrel, "this is Grandmother Bear. She has seen many sunrises and lived through many a cold, snowy winter. She is wise in the ways of the woods. Perhaps she can answer your questions."

Tessa hopped down to a low branch where she could look right into the eyes of Grandmother Bear. They were warm and kindly. They looked up at Tessa with tenderness. "Yes," said Grandmother Bear, "I have come because my friend Squirrel tells me you are quite sad. He tells me you miss your father so far away. And he says you are worried that your father might forget you." Tessa nodded, a tear coming to her eye. Grandmother Bear smiled knowingly, then continued. "My child, perhaps you do not understand the depths of a father's love. It is as bottomless as the seven oceans; it is as wide and open as the endless sky. It is as enduring as the purple mountains and as gentle and caressing as the whispering wind. Perhaps your father will grow to love others, perhaps he will even love another child. But you alone are his daughter. His love for you lives in a special part of his heart. It will never die but only grow with each passing year, no matter if you are close or far apart."

Tessa hopped down to a low branch where she could look right into the eyes of Grandmother Bear. They were warm and kindly. They looked up at Tessa with tenderness.

Tessa blinked away a few tears. Her sadness started to melt. She felt a warm sensation in her stomach where just before had been a tight knot. She thanked her friend Squirrel and Grandmother Bear. She had to get home for dinner. Her mother and the other birds would be waiting. When she got back to Mama's nest, there was some mail waiting for her. It was a letter from Papa bird. He wrote that he missed her and thought about her a lot. There was a picture of Papa and Tessa hugging. She hung it right by her bed. It made her smile to remember how that hug had felt. And to remember how all the rest of Papa's hugs would feel for many years to come.

CHAPTER 3

Robbie Rabbit

JANET JOHNSTON

Children often harbor reunion fantasies about their divorced parents and fail to grasp that divorce is an adult issue for which children are not responsible. This story helps children by addressing a variety of tactics and approaches about which they might fantasize. The story encourages children to disengage from the parental issues and go on with their own developmental tasks, while knowing that their parents will be united in their mutual pride in their children's achievements.

Chapter 1

Robbie was a smart little brown rabbit with long, floppy ears and a cute white tail. He had large, bright brown eyes and a sweet smile. Everyone who knew him liked him very much. Robbie Rabbit was also very good with words. He often talked to his Mom and his Dad about lots of good ideas. Sometimes he played with his friends and made up great adventure stories in which they pretended they were Ninja turtles.

Robbie's Mom had a little house in a deep burrow under a large oak tree near the river. Robbie's Dad lived over the hill in another burrow where there were a whole lot of houses joined together. Sometimes Robbie lived with his Mom and sometimes he lived with his Dad.

Robbie led a very, very busy life. Each morning he had to get up and brush his teeth and groom his fur. Sometimes he had to go out to the field with his Mom to dig for fresh carrots. Sometimes he had to go to the river with his Dad to get some fresh water. Sometimes his Mom had to go to help her friends with their work, and Robbie Rabbit would have to go along too. And then, of course, Robbie had to go to school each day to practice running fast and to learn how to make things and to sing and dance with his friends.

Now, Robbie liked to sit in the sun and smell the flowers. He liked to make up stories with his toys and spend the whole day just playing in his bedroom at his Mom's house. He liked to spend the whole day quietly with his Dad watching beetles in the yard at his Dad's house. Often he liked to just sit and watch TV.

"Come on, Robbie, we have to go to the library," his Mom would call. "Hurry, Robbie, we'll be late for school!" or "If we don't leave soon, we'll miss your doctor's appointment!" All the time, it seemed as though Robbie had to go somewhere. And when he got somewhere, then he had to go somewhere else! "Now it's time to go to your Dad's house, Robbie. Quickly, get your things ready!"

Robbie was upset. Everything was happening just too fast. There were always too many things to do! So he decided to slow down and stop. He didn't brush his teeth or groom his hair when he got up in the morning. He ate his breakfast very, very slowly, until it was too late to go out into the field to dig for carrots. When it came time to practice his running, he sat down on the floor and held on to the kitchen table and said, "No!" When he had to leave for school, he held on to the bed. Robbie Rabbit started to hold on to everything. He held on to the chair, he held on to the TV, he held on to the gate, and he even held on to his Mom's leg. Robbie Rabbit started to say "No!" to everything. He said "No!" to his breakfast, and "No!" to his dinner, and "No!" to going to bed. He even said "No!" to playing with his friends. He just stayed home and stayed in bed!

After a while Robbie Rabbit got very bored. There was nothing to do in bed all day. He was lonely. There were no friends to play with in his bedroom. He forgot how to run fast and his legs became wobbly. He began to grow small and thin because he didn't eat his breakfast and dinner. He became tired of sitting on the floor and watching TV.

One beautiful sunny morning, he looked out the window and said to his Mom, "Let's go on an adventure today. Let's go see my good friend Roger Rabbit." So off they went. He had a wonderful day playing with his friends, running in the fields, swimming in the river, and

When he had to leave for school, he held on to the bed. Robbie Rabbit started to hold on to everything.

digging for juicy new carrots. When he came home, he was starving and he ate a huge dinner. The next morning he woke up to find he had grown two inches bigger and his legs were strong and healthy again. He decided to go to school to practice his running and to learn how to read and write and dance and sing with his friends. Robbie Rabbit told his Mom and Dad, "It's *much* better to do lots of fun things each day!"

Chapter 2

Robbie Rabbit was cross and tired and sad and mad! Every few days he had to brush his fur coat, put on his running shoes, pack his carrots, and leave his Mom's burrow under the oak tree and go over the hill to his Dad's burrow. He cried when he left his Mom because he really missed her. He missed the quiet talks and the cuddles they had together. Robbie was with his Dad only a few days when he had to brush his fur coat, put on his running shoes, pack his carrots, and leave his Dad's burrow and go back over the hill to his Mom's burrow. He was sad when he left his Dad because he really missed him. He missed the fun times they had looking for lizards and bugs and building sand castles together.

Back and forth! Back and forth! Mom's house, Dad's house, Mom's house, Dad's house.

One day, Robbie yelled angrily, "Why can't my Mom and Dad live in the same burrow so I can see them both every day? Why can't they be friends?" And Robbie Rabbit sat down in the middle of the path and refused to budge. "Come on, Robbie," said his Mom, "time to go to school!"

"No!" said Robbie, and he lay down on the path. Just then his nice teacher, Ms. Teresa Rabbit, came skipping along. She stopped when she saw Robbie lying on his back in the middle of the path. "What's the matter, Robbie?" she asked. "Why are you lying here looking so cross and tired and sad and mad?"

"Why can't my Mom and Dad live in the same burrow so I can see them both every day? Why can't they be friends?" cried Robbie.

Ms. Teresa, his kind teacher, sat down next to the small brown bunny and said, "I think I need to tell you a story, Robbie." This is the story she told Robbie:

"A long time ago, before you were born, your Mommy was a beautiful dancer. Every day she danced and danced. She was very pretty, with brown eyes just like yours. Your Daddy was also very clever because he built wonderful castles in the sand. Every day he built castles that looked like poetry. He was very handsome, just like you. When your Mommy and Daddy met, they loved each other very much. They decided to make a family together in one burrow.

"Very soon a dear little brown bunny with a cute white tail was born. This was you, Robbie Rabbit. You were smart and clever just like your Mom and Dad. Your Mommy and Daddy loved you very much.

"But then there was trouble in this family of rabbits. You see, Mommy Rabbit was a quiet, timid rabbit and she liked to play and dance by herself. Daddy Rabbit was a bold rabbit and he wanted to play with Mommy all the time. When Mommy danced, Daddy tried to do his dance. 'Stop it!'

"No!" said Robbie, and he lay down on the path. Just then his nice teacher, Ms. Teresa Rabbit, came skipping along. She stopped when she saw Robbie lying in the middle of the path. "What's the matter, Robbie?" she asked.

Mommy cried, 'You messed up my dance!' When Mommy
Rabbit painted pictures, Daddy Rabbit tried to paint too.
'Stop it! You messed up my picture,' she cried. When
Daddy Rabbit built his wonderful sand castles, he wanted
Mommy Rabbit to watch him build them. 'No!' said
Mommy, 'I want to run and dance in the sunshine.' 'Stop!
Come back here!' Daddy Rabbit was getting angry. 'No!
Leave me alone,' said Mommy Rabbit. She was getting
angry too. So they argued and argued and fought. Mommy
Rabbit spent most of the day hiding and Daddy Rabbit
spent most of the day looking for her. She was scared and
angry. He was lonely and angry. They were both so un-
happy that they decided to live in different burrows.

"Since they both loved you so much, Robbie Rabbit, it
was decided that you should live some days with your
Mommy and some days with your Daddy. You see, Robbie Rabbit, your Mommy and Daddy are two different
kinds of rabbits. Mommy Rabbit likes to do things mostly
by herself in her own way. Daddy Rabbit likes to do
things with Mommy and he wants to do things his way.
So when they lived together in the same burrow, they just
argued and fought all the time. Everyone was unhappy.

"But you, Robbie Rabbit, you are half like your
Mommy and half like your Daddy. You like to play by
yourself and you like to be with your friends. You love to
run and dance and build castles in the sand. You can live
in your Mom's burrow and you can live in your Dad's
burrow! And your Mommy will *always* be there when
you come back to her burrow! And your Daddy will *always* be there when you come back to his burrow!"

Robbie Rabbit smiled and stood up in the path. Now he understood why his parents couldn't live together in the same burrow. He put his small brown paw in his teacher's soft paw and they skipped together all the way to school.

Chapter 3

Robbie Rabbit was growing bigger and bigger. He was going to school every day and learning how to read and write. He also learned how to draw wonderful pictures and tell good stories. Every day after school he gathered sticks and stones around the burrows and built wonderful inventions—super robots and space vehicles. He was a very, very busy bunny!

Sometimes he played with his friends at school, sometimes he was with his Mom in her burrow under the old oak tree, and sometimes he was with his Dad in his burrow over the hill.

His Mom loved him very much with a mother-bunny-love, and his Dad loved him very much with a father-bunny-love. Robbie Rabbit loved both his Mom and Dad very much. And how he wished they could all be together!

One day he sat down in the tall grass and thought and thought and thought about how he could bring his Mom and Dad together. He thought up all kinds of plans.

His first plan was to play a trick on his parents. When Daddy Rabbit called to talk to him on the phone at his Mom's burrow, Robbie Rabbit said, "Someone wants to talk to you on the phone, Mom."

Mommy picked up the phone. "Hello," she said.

"Hello," said Daddy.

"What do you want?" Mommy asked.

"I want to talk to Robbie Rabbit," Daddy answered.

So Mommy gave the phone back to Robbie without saying another word. Robbie Rabbit was disappointed. That plan didn't work at all!

His second plan was to have a party. He made two glasses of carrot juice and two plates of fresh lettuce, and he decorated the table with two big red balloons. Then he called his Mom and invited her to his party. Then he called his Dad and invited him to his party. When they both came, he said "Surprise!" His Mom and Dad looked at each other.

"I think there must be some mistake," Daddy Rabbit said politely. "I came to have a party with Robbie Rabbit, not with you. "

"Yes, I think there has been a mistake," Mommy Rabbit agreed. "I came to have a party with Robbie Rabbit, not with you. You can have your party with Robbie now, and I'll have my party with Robbie later." And Mommy Rabbit left without another word. Robbie Rabbit was disappointed. That plan didn't work either!

His next plan was to pretend to be sick. One morning when he woke at his Dad's burrow, he moaned and groaned. "OOH! AAH! I have a tummyache! OOH! AAH! I have a headache! OOH! AAH! My feet hurt!" Daddy Rabbit was worried.

"You'd better call my Mommy on the phone," Robbie Rabbit said, "Ask her to come over right away!"

"I need to call Doctor Dinosaur, not your mother," Daddy Rabbit said. Doctor Dinosaur told Robbie he needed to lie still in bed all day. Robbie Rabbit couldn't go to school that day, and he couldn't play with his friends. He was bored, bored, bored! Now he was really frustrated! That plan didn't work either!

Robbie Rabbit was getting mad! This was stupid! Why couldn't his parents be together? Sometimes he felt it was Mommy Rabbit's fault. One day he got angry and kicked and kicked the oak tree at his mother's burrow. He kicked so hard that he broke his toe! It was bleeding so badly that he got very scared and Mommy Rabbit got very scared. They called the ambulance and rushed to the hospital. Daddy Rabbit heard about the accident and he rushed to the hospital, too.

While Doctor Dinosaur stitched up Robbie's toe, Mommy Rabbit stood on one side of the bed holding one of Robbie's paws and Daddy Rabbit stood on the other side of the bed, holding the other paw. Robbie was so pleased! At last his Mommy and Daddy were both together with him!

Next day, Robbie told his nice teacher, Ms. Teresa Rabbit, how he had at last found a way of bringing his Mommy and Daddy together. "But Robbie!" cried Ms. Teresa, "You can't hurt yourself just to bring your Mom and Dad together! That would be a terrible thing to do."

Robbie looked at his toe with the big bandage, and he thought about how it hurt, and how he was so scared when he saw the blood. His teacher was right; he couldn't just hurt himself so that his Mom and Dad could be together. Teacher Teresa Rabbit and Mommy Rabbit and Daddy Rabbit all agreed: Robbie shouldn't hurt himself just so he could have his parents together.

They all had a big talk to come up with a better plan. Mommy Rabbit explained that she just was not comfortable being with Daddy Rabbit. He was a different kind of rabbit and he liked playing different kinds of games. Daddy Rabbit said that he didn't feel comfortable being with Mommy Rabbit because she was a different kind of rabbit and she liked playing different kinds of games.

Then Mommy and Daddy Rabbit agreed on one important thing. They both loved Robbie Rabbit. They both loved to go to his school and see his reading and writing and his wonderful pictures and his good stories. They both loved to watch him play and sing and dance with his rabbit friends at his school. This was one place where they could all be together from time to time, and everyone would be safe and happy.

CHAPTER 4

The Lions of Africa

JANET JOHNSTON

Some parents divorce because they simply grow into separate lives and identities over the years. This may happen when a mother begins a career or profession and finds a new sense of herself, or when one parent grows older or less interested in activities that were previously enjoyed together. "The Lions of Africa" offers a solution for an older child experiencing his parents' growing not only apart but growing in different directions. For some children, the solution is through emancipation by joining with a peer group that represents some of the best features of each parent.

Far, far away on the great plains of central Africa, where the sun burns hot and wild animals roam free, there lived a magnificent lion. He was strong and powerful and a capable hunter and a fiercely independent thinker. He was so strong and so swift that he was really not afraid of any-one or anything.

Even though he made some mistakes when he was young, over the years he became very wise and felt so strong and confident in himself that he began to take care of the weaker and smaller animals. He lived alone many years, just watching out for his animal neighbors until he met and fell in love with a beautiful young lioness. She was spirited and loving, but a little afraid and really depended on the great lion for protection. Sometime later, their young son was born—a splendid, tough little fun-loving male cub. The great lion enjoyed caring for and protecting his family. He hunted and brought home good food while the mother lioness nursed her baby cub in the den. These were happy times in this family of lions. When the young cub became older, many times in the early hours of the morning before the sun became too hot, the lion family would go on hunting expeditions together. The father would teach his young son to hunt small prey with skill and patience. The mother lioness, although she was more strict and would stand no nonsense, showed him places to play hide-and-go-seek and took him to swimming holes in which to swim with other young cubs.

As the magnificent lion grew older, he was still strong, though he was quieter and liked to spend more time lying in the sun. He was gentle and wise. He did not have to fight anymore to protect his family and provide for them because he was well respected in his territory.

But the beautiful younger lioness mother was not ready to lie in the sun with her mate. She did not feel timid anymore and did not need his protection. She wanted to go on hunting expeditions herself, with some of her many lion friends. The great lion and lioness began to squabble and fight between themselves. Sometimes they wrestled with each other, and the lion cub, who was a young teenager at this stage, was either ignored in the hassle or at times was actually bitten in the fray. It was not a particularly happy situation. Gradually the lioness began to spend most of her time living in another den several miles away. The magnificent old lion, with his flowing golden mane, was quite sad and rather lonely but realized it was best to live as they did.

Now the young male cub was becoming strong and powerful and more independent himself, but he was not ready for his family to split up like this. He liked the family expeditions they used to have. He felt kind of mad at his parents for not trying harder to make it work, and then he was kind of sad and lonely at times.

When he was with one parent, he missed the other parent. He felt like growling and biting and snarling, but he knew no one would like him if he did that. So instead he sat very still and tried very, very hard to be good. When he felt sad, he tried not to think about it. He did not practice his fighting and hunting so much because he was scared that his real feelings would come out and he would become too angry and really hurt someone.

The wise old lion, even though he knew how his son was feeling, did not say much. Instead he encouraged his young protégé to wrestle and play with other young male cubs a great deal. The lioness was concerned too. She re-

The great lion and lioness began to squabble and fight between themselves. Sometimes they wrestled with each other, and the lion cub, who was a young teenager at this stage, was either ignored in the hassle or at times was actually bitten in the fray.

ally wanted her young son to get on with his life and not take too much notice of the fight between the parents.

Gradually the young male cub began to do just that. As he grew older, he spent more and more time with other young male lions, and even romped with young lionesses at times. He grew to become even stronger and a better hunter than his father because he learned not only all of his father's courage and hunting skills but also acquired his mother's energy and love of adventure.

CHAPTER 5

Claudio and Petra

JANET JOHNSTON

Following the separation, it is not uncommon for one or both parents to experience feelings of sadness and helplessness. Some parents fail to take care of themselves, and without consciously realizing it they put their children in the role of caretaker. Scared and worried about their parents' well-being, children will readily assume this role and sacrifice their own needs for those of their parents. These children need permission to resume the role of being the child in the family, and they also need assurances that both their parents are grown-ups who know how to take care of themselves.

Far, far away in the North Pole, among all the snow and ice, lived a large white polar bear. His name was Claudio. Claudio had a hard life. He had to hunt all day and sometimes fish all night for food. He lived all by himself in a big ice cave. Claudio's best friend was a little dog called Petra, who would come to visit him. Although Claudio was very large and Petra was quite small, the two animals loved to romp and play together in the snow during the wintertime and go on expeditions together in the soft summer sunshine.

When the weather was stormy, Claudio worried a lot about finding enough food to eat. Sometimes when Petra visited, she found her big friend kind of sad and lonely. Now, Petra was a very kind little dog with a big heart, and she decided she would take care of her big friend. Petra worked all day and all night looking for food and brought Claudio some fish to eat. She tried to think up some fun new games to play to make him happy.

But the big polar bear needed a lot of food to eat and the little dog could carry only a little bit of food in her mouth. Little Petra worked harder and harder. When Claudio cried tears, Petra tried to be very brave and cheer him up. She could never show her big friend that she was sometimes sad, too. Petra worked so hard that she became very tired and worried herself.

The big white polar bear noticed how his little friend was changing. He decided to have a heart-to-heart talk with her. "Petra, you are my very good friend. I love to have you come and visit me. We have wonderful times together. But I don't want you to worry about finding my food. I'm big and strong and I can really look after myself. Sure, I complain sometimes but that's just because I like to say exactly what I think. And sure, I cry sometimes, but that's because I like to do exactly what I feel like doing when I am sad. And sure, I am lonely sometimes, but I

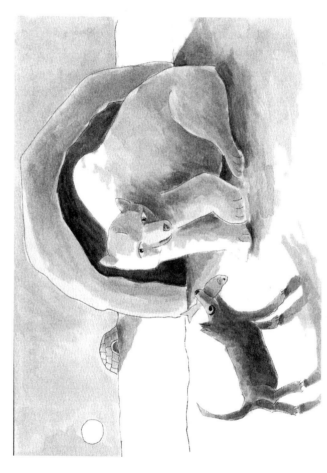

Petra worked all day and all night looking for food and brought Claudio some fish to eat.

have other polar bears to visit for company. I can really look after myself. I am big and you are only small. I want you to be my good friend and I want us to have fun together. When you feel happy, I want you to laugh, and when you feel sad, I want you to feel free to cry!"

Little Petra was so relieved! She stopped working so hard and became a much happier little dog. Petra continued to visit her big friend, Claudio, but she spent time playing with other little doggy friends too.

CHAPTER 6

The Dancers

KAREN BREUNIG

Some children of divorce experience one or both parents entering into a new relationship, possibly one that leads to remarriage and the creation of a step-family. "The Dancers" explores this theme in a gentle way, helping children to put aside their resentment, replacing it with the joy and growth that can be found in experiencing new things in life.

Once upon a time, long ago, there was a little girl who loved to dance. Now, this was not surprising as both her mother and her father were dancers. In fact, most everyone in her family—her brother, her grandparents, cousins, aunts, and uncles—were dancers of great renown throughout the small kingdom where they lived. Her family made their living dancing. They performed in their gaily colored costumes of reds, blues, and greens. Their long, golden scarves sparkled in the sunlight. They often danced at the royal court and at festivals and fairs.

As the little girl grew older, her parents and brother began to teach her their dances. Some of the dances she knew already. She had watched them since she was a baby. Others were a little more complicated and took her months of practice. There were many steps to remember, and the dancers had to know when to move together as if they were one and when to move alone. They had to know how to move to different kinds of music. Some music made them happy and energetic. Other music made them feel sad and slow. They had to learn to watch the others and their movements at the same time they had to decide what movements they should make and when.

The little girl was an eager learner. She watched her parents and her brother carefully. She practiced every day. She loved her mother's fluid, graceful style. It fit well with her own movements. She loved her father's energetic, sweeping gestures. They made her feel bold. And she loved her brother's precise, careful steps. Sometimes he made her giggle to herself because he could be so serious. But what she liked best were those days when they danced as if they were one person with four moving parts.

Now, this did not happen every day. It didn't even happen every week. And lately it seemed to the little girl that it was happening less and less. Her parents were struggling to stay in rhythm. Her father's bold gestures didn't seem to be working anymore with her mother's graceful ones. They were always stepping on each other's toes and tripping over each other's feet. The little girl could see the frustration on their faces. She could see their disappointment and anger. And she began to worry.

One rainy afternoon, her parents came to the girl as she was practicing some new steps. She hoped that somehow the new steps would make her parents happy. The girl's parents approached slowly, with sadness in their eyes. "Your father and I have made a big decision," her mother said. "It seems that as we have grown older, our dancing styles have changed. Your father's bold style and my flowing style are not working as they once did. We are only tripping each other up and preventing ourselves from being the kind of dancers we would like to be. We have decided to dance separately." Her dad continued, "We will form two new dance troupes, one with you, your mom, and your brother, and one with you, me, and your brother."

The girl's eyes filled with tears. "Maybe if we learned some new dances, some easier steps, maybe that would help?" she said. "Maybe if brother and I learn some new steps or learn to dance better. Maybe it is just us." The tears were now rolling down her cheeks. "I do not know how to dance in a troupe with three. I only know dances that are for four." Now she was sobbing. Her parents took turns holding her and trying to comfort her. They cried, too. Then, in their frustration, they began to blame each other. "It is your fault that you do not dance boldly like me," her father yelled at her mother. "You could change if you wanted to. You are just stubborn." "You do not understand me. You never have. You only think of yourself," the mother yelled back. "Please stop. Please stop," the little girl cried out. She thought her heart might break.

Time passed and two new dance troupes were formed. At night, the little girl dreamed longingly of those days when the four of them danced as if they were one. During the day, she began the hard work of learning new dances for three. Some weeks she danced with her father and brother, the bold, sweeping dances that her father loved. Other weeks she and her brother practiced with their mother the graceful, flowing movements their mother was so good at. After some time, new dances took shape, dances that were meant just for three. They got back their rhythm. They got back their knack for moving together when it was called for. They started to remember how to move to the music. The sad music touched the girl's heart in the place that still longed for her parents to be partners again. When the sad music played, she danced with tears in her eyes. The happy music seemed harder to move to. She tried to find joy in the dance itself, or in knowing that her mother, father, and brother still loved her. The love had not stopped. That was comforting. Nor had the dancing. That was comforting, too. But she missed the joy of four dancers moving together.

Word spread throughout the land that the famous dancing family was once again performing, but now they were two troupes instead of one. The people called them the Mother Dancers and the Father Dancers. They were happy to see that the children were in both troupes, for the children danced well with both their mother and their father. And they were delighted to see that their dancing was exciting and beautiful once again. The people did notice that the dances were not the same as before. Dances for three are very different from dances for four. As time passed, the audiences grew to love the new dances as much as they had the old ones. And the girl grew to love them too.

Both the Mother Dancers and the Father Dancers were traveling the land dancing at festivals, fairs, castles, and the royal court. Each troupe had new costumes. The Mother Dancers' costumes were purple and yellow with green stripes and beautiful embroidery down the front. The girl's skirt billowed in the breeze as she spun around. The Father Dancers wore costumes of red and blue stripes with wide gold sashes. The children's lives were very busy. They became very skilled at fitting in with Dad's style when they were with him, and Mom's style when they were with her. As the girl grew older, her dancing grew better. She became more aware of her own rhythm. She could feel the music in her bones. Her dancing was bolder. She was more graceful. Her steps grew more confident. Time passed and the Mother Dancers and the Father Dancers became known throughout the kingdom as the two best dancing troupes.

One evening, the mother came to the girl as she rested in bed reading. "My daughter," she said, "I feel our troupe is too small. I yearn to dance again with a partner. We need to add another to our troupe so that we may do the dances for four again." The girl's heart skipped a beat. "This must mean she and my father are going to dance together again," she thought. She felt joy rising up in her chest. "Oh, yes, mother! That is a great idea. When will we be four again?" Her mother was smiling. "I have met a man who is one of the finest dancers in the land. His name is Ian. He has agreed to dance with us. His style is a good match for mine. We will make good partners. He will join us next month when we dance at the royal court."

The girl felt her heart drop in her chest. The joy leaked out of her like air from a balloon. Her eyes teared up. Her face got hot and red. Her mother noticed. "What is it, my girl?" she asked. "Why do you look so sad when only a minute ago you looked delighted?"

"I will not dance with anyone who is not my family," she said angrily. "I will not do the dances for four with a stranger. I don't want this stranger in our troupe." Now she was shouting. "If he is not my father, I do not want to dance with him." She buried her head in her pillow and sobbed. Her mother tried to comfort her, but the girl pushed her away. That night the girl dreamed longingly of the old days. She awoke with a heavy heart. She could not dance that day, nor for many days that followed. Her mother and her brother tried to comfort her. They sang to her and told her jokes. They brought her gifts. They urged her to come and walk in the woods with them. Nothing seemed to help.

The mother was growing worried. The day when they were to dance in the royal court was coming fast. The girl refused to practice as a foursome. She knew this new dancer would not dance like her father. His style was different. His movements were not as bold and quick. He was slower, more thoughtful, and careful. She didn't think she would know how to dance with him. Watching him dance with her smiling mother only made her miss her father more. It was true that they danced well together. They were graceful and confident. Her mother seemed happier than she had been in a long time. The girl was angry that her mother was happy while she was so sad. Yet it was also good to see her mother happy. She felt so confused. Her head felt as if she had done too many spins.

The day of the royal performance arrived. The Mother Dancers dressed in their finest costumes. They wove golden threads through their hair. The girl reluctantly practiced a few steps with the others. The newest member smiled at her, but she refused to look him in the eye. He and her mother were dancing well together. Her brother had learned some new dances to do with them. He too was dancing well. She felt as if she was the only one with a heavy heart and heavy feet to match.

The crowd at the royal court was warm and welcoming. They were eager to see how the dance troupe would perform with its new member. Mother and Ian began the dance. Brother soon joined in. The music was lively. The dance was going well, with only a few small missteps. Then the girl joined them. She began on the wrong foot. Her mind was racing, "Should I go left or right? Do I circle in back of my brother or in front? I will not take that man's hand. I can't dance with him. He's too different." She put her foot out and tripped him as he passed. He landed right on his face in front of the king and queen. The crowd gasped. Then there was a long silence. He arose and bowed to the royal couple. He took her mother's hand and continued where he had left off. Only this time he refused to take the girl's hand, and he glanced at her every time she passed.

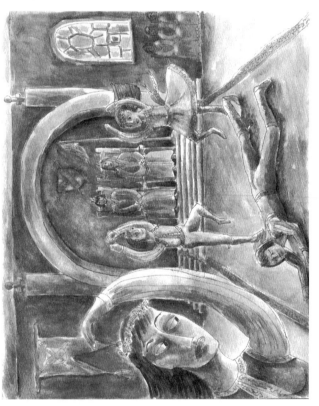

Then the girl joined them. She began on the wrong foot. Her mind was racing, "Should I go left or right? Do I circle in back of my brother or in front? I will not take that man's hand. I can't dance with him. He's too different." She put her foot out and tripped him as he passed. He landed right on his face in front of the king and queen.

Mother's radiant smile had faded. She was concentrating on keeping them apart. The dance ended, the crowd applauded politely, and the troupe silently headed for home.

Weeks passed. Ian refused to speak with the girl. She began to feel sorry for what she had done. "Perhaps I could learn one or two dances to do with him," she thought. There were certain movements that he was very good at. She liked how he lifted her mother into the air. Maybe he would do that with her. But she didn't want to dance with him the way she danced with her father. She couldn't do the Father Dances with him. She was certain of that.

She tried to talk to Ian. He ignored her and spoke only with her brother and mother. He scolded her for missing a step during rehearsal, for dancing too fast or too slow. Her mother would stop rehearsal and take Ian aside. They would talk in hushed tones with angry looks on their faces. The girl worried her dancing would never suit him. If he left their troupe, it would make her mother sad and lonely again. Ian and her mother were dancing so well together. The joy had returned to her mother's step. She didn't want that to disappear.

One day, as they rehearsed in the meadow, Ian softened toward her. He turned to her with a slight smile and said, "I like how you are moving your arms and hands in this dance. It is very graceful and lively. You are very good at this dance." She felt some warmth stir in her heart. "Perhaps he does like my dancing after all," she thought. Her mother patted her on the back and smiled at Ian.

Their next performance, at the county fair, went very well. They knew their steps and moved gracefully in rhythm with one another and the music. The crowd was enthusiastic. The new dances for four were finally working.

The girl's grandmother had been watching from the crowd, as she often did. Grandmother came to the girl after the dance and congratulated her. "You are dancing so well, my dear granddaughter. Those were beautiful dances, and so intricate," she said.

"They are different from those we danced with my mother and father," the girl replied. "It has been hard learning these new dances. It feels as if we are always changing our dances. First, dances for four, then dances for three, and now dances for four again, but different ones. I would like to have our dances stay the same. I am tired of so many changes."

The grandmother looked warmly at the girl. "My child, change is the very nature of dance. No dance is ever done twice in exactly the same way. When we are small and our dance is that of a small child, we feel it will always be the same. We know a few small steps and we dance them with our families. We think we will never need to know other steps. It is a grand illusion. As you grow, and your body gets stronger and more sure of itself, it can take on many new, exciting, and sometimes scary steps. And you can learn to dance with many different people. There is much that other dancers have to teach you. But you must let go of the small child's idea that you can dance the same dance over and over again in the same way. That will only keep you stuck."

"But what if I like those old dances?" the girl asked. "What if I don't want to leave them behind?"

"You never really leave them behind," Grandmother replied. "They will always be a part of you. You will carry them in your heart. And you will find that the steps of your old dances will find their way into your new dances. They will get reborn again and again. It is as if the old dances were golden threads and you are using them to weave a beautiful tapestry. If golden threads were all you used, there would be no image on the tapestry. But woven with other colorful threads, they form a beautiful picture."

Grandmother put her arm around the girl. They stayed quietly together for a few minutes. Then the girl jumped to her feet with a smile on her face. She pulled at Grandmother's hand. "Grandmother, will you teach me that dance you used to do with my mother? The one where you danced in a circle, then danced alone, then came back together again?"

"Certainly," Grandmother said. She took the girl's hands and formed a circle. Soon they were lost in the dance.

PART II

High-Conflict Divorce Concerns

CHAPTER 7

The Giraffe Who Couldn't Speak

JANET JOHNSTON

Some children caught in loyalty conflicts between their parents cope through profound withdrawal and a fear of speaking or expressing their own opinions. Many of these children eventually compromise so much of their functioning that they fail to develop a sense of individual identity. Sometimes the only solution is for complete disengagement between the parents and for the child to have permission to form a separate relationship with each parent.

Far, far away on the plains of Africa lived many wild and wonderful animals. There were lions, tigers, elephants, zebras, deer, rhinoceros, and giraffes.

Gerri Giraffe was a beautiful and graceful animal with a long, long neck and long, long legs. She loved to wander among the tall trees and chew the sweet new green leaves. Gerri had two very special friends whom she loved very much. One friend was Lilli Lion and the other friend was Teddi Tiger. Gerri liked to go on adventures with Teddi Tiger, and she also liked to sit in the sun and chat with Lilli Lion.

But there was one problem. Teddi Tiger and Lilli Lion did not like each other. Every time they met, they started to argue. "The grass is green," said Lilli. "No! The grass is yellow," snapped Teddi. And so they argued and argued.

Gerri Giraffe was sad. She liked both her friends Teddi Tiger *and* Lilli Lion. When they came to play with her, they always ended up in an argument. Sometimes they growled and snapped and bit each other. Sometimes they chased each other and caused such a great commotion that all the other animals also started fighting.

Teddi Tiger would say to Gerri Giraffe, "Let's go on a wonderful adventure." Lilli Lion would argue, "She doesn't want to do that. Gerri wants to sit with me in the sun." Gerri Giraffe didn't want to hurt her friends' feelings and she didn't want them to start arguing, so she closed her mouth and didn't say anything.

Then Teddi Tiger would say, "My friend Gerri likes to eat sycamore leaves." "No she doesn't," argued Lilli, "She likes to eat oak leaves." Gerri Giraffe didn't want to hurt her friends' feelings and she didn't want them to start fighting, so she didn't say anything. She decided not to eat any leaves at all.

Then Lilli Lion said, "My friend Gerri Giraffe wants to wear a yellow jacket like mine." "No, dummy! My friend Gerri wants to wear a black-striped jacket like mine," argued Teddi Tiger. Gerri Giraffe closed her mouth and didn't say anything. She really liked her own mottled jacket, but she didn't want to hurt her friends' feelings and she hated it when they fought.

Very soon, something strange happened. Gerri Giraffe had stopped talking for so long that she forgot how to speak. When a new neighbor, Zilli Zebra, moved in and asked, "What's your name?" Gerri could only say, "H H H H H Hi, m m m m m m m my n n n n n n n name i i i i i i i i i i i i i i i i . . ." She couldn't say anything more!

Teddi Tiger and Lilli Lion were worried. They decided to take Gerri Giraffe to Doctor Dinosaur to find out what the problem was. Doctor Dinosaur took out a long, long spoon and asked Gerri to open her mouth. He looked down her long, long throat with a flashlight. "Seems OK," he said, puzzled.

Just then Lilli Lion said, "I know what the problem is. Gerri went on a long adventure with Teddi Tiger and she got wet and caught a cold." "That's stupid," said Teddi. "The problem is that Gerri got too hot lying in the sun with Lilli Lion and now she has a fever." And both Lilli and Teddi began to argue and fight again, right in Doctor Dinosaur's office!

"I can see what the problem is now," said Doctor Dinosaur, and he quickly wrote out a prescription on his white pad. This is what it said:

Prescription for Gerri Giraffe

In the morning, Gerri should take one glass of water
and play with her friend Teddi Tiger.
In the evening, Gerri should take one glass of water
and play with her friend Lilli Lion.

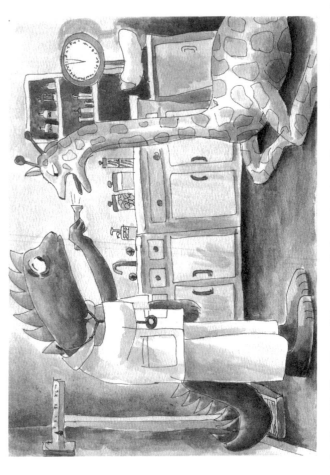

They decided to take Gerri Giraffe to Doctor Dinosaur to find out what the problem was. Doctor Dinosaur took out a long, long spoon and asked Gerri to open her mouth. He looked down her long, long, long throat with a flashlight. "Seems OK," he said, puzzled.

All the rest of the day, Gerri should go to school
and play with all her other friends, the elephants,
zebras, deer, rhinoceros.
Then she will be able to talk and sing and dance
without hearing any arguments.

And sure enough, as soon as Gerri Giraffe played with
her other friends, she found she could talk again. "What's
your name?" asked Zilli Zebra. "Hi, my name is Gerri
Giraffe, and I like to eat all kinds of leaves. I like to wear a
mottled jacket, and I like to go on adventures and sit in
the sun!" she said happily.

CHAPTER 8

Hector Horse

JANET JOHNSTON

*Children exposed to high-conflict divorce and loy-
alty binds over time are likely to adopt maladaptive
patterns. Most at risk is the loss of a sense of being
in touch with their own feelings in an attempt to
meet the needs of their parents. The following story
assists children in reconciling parents with different
value systems. It teaches children that both parents
may be right from their own perspectives and that
the children can, in time, define their own value systems based on what their parents have presented.*

Chapter 1
Hector and Felicity

Once upon a time, in a beautiful country by the sea, there
lived a strong, handsome, brown horse called Hector. When
Hector Horse was young, he had many friends. They played

together and had wonderful adventures and sometimes even got into mischief. Now, Hector Horse was a clever horse and he was a working horse. He decided he really needed to work very hard and make a nice home for himself and not just play around all day. So for many years he worked and worked and worked, pulling the plow to till the land to make fertile fields, and dragging piles of wood together to build a home. Finally, when he was more than thirty years old, Hector Horse built a beautiful barn with a big haystack filled with hay to eat in the wintertime, and beautiful fields of green grass to eat in the summertime. He loved his home, but he found he was very lonely. He decided he needed to look for a lady horse to be his wife.

Hector Horse went to the fair one day, and there he met a lot of very nice lady horses. There was Jane and Betty and Mary, all strong lady horses that were about his age. They would all make good wives and they were all ready to get married. Just as he was trying to make up his mind which one to marry, Hector Horse suddenly saw the prettiest little filly that he ever did see! Her name was Felicity Filly, and she had a white silky coat and black silk mane and tail! She danced and pranced and whinnied and neighed so that everyone watched her. Hector Horse fell in love with her almost immediately. He wanted her for his wife.

Now, the problem was that Felicity Filly was a *very* young pony, just a teenager. She didn't know too much about the world. She was just practicing falling in love, as teenagers often do. She thought it was wonderful when this strong, brown, older horse called Hector took notice of her and gave her lots of presents. She was happy when he told her he loved her. She imagined she was in love with him, too. So when Hector Horse asked her to marry him, Felicity Filly said "Yes" right away, and they got married. Soon, Felicity Filly had three beautiful baby foals. She and Hector called their babies Sena, Marnie, and Tisa.

Hector Horse was a very proud father and Felicity Filly loved her babies. She tried to be a good wife and a good mother. But she was often tired and cross and lonely. She missed her other teenage friends a lot. She was a bit envious when she saw her friends playing together and going to fairs while she had to stay at home. The problem was that Felicity Filly was just a teenager. She was not ready to get married. She needed to do much more practicing falling in love and playing with friends. Felicity Filly began to get cross and irritable and have lots of little arguments and fights with Hector Horse.

Hector Horse tried very hard to make Felicity Filly happy. He dug with his hoofs and made a nice big swimming hole for her and the baby foals. He took his family for a vacation by the ocean, and they all pranced along the seashore. But Felicity Filly became more and more unhappy. Hector Horse was a grown-up, older horse. He was ready to be a husband and a daddy. He wanted to work hard and bring home food and presents to his beautiful young filly wife and his cute baby foals, Sena, Marnie, and Tisa.

One day, Felicity Filly had a big fight with Hector Horse and then she said, "I'm leaving! I can't live with you anymore. I don't want to be married! I want to play with my friends, and I want to practice falling in love with other young horses!"

Hector Horse was first very surprised, and then he was very sad and very, very disappointed. He was also quite angry with Felicity Filly. He said, "You have broken your promise! OK, you can go, but you have to leave the baby foals with me. I want to look after Sena, Marnie, and Tisa. I am a good father, and I love my children. You can go and play with your friends, but the babies stay here!"

"Oh, no! No! No!" cried Felicity Filly. "I love my little foals. I want to look after them myself. I will be a good mother to them. You can just visit them. They need to live with me because I am the mother!"

And so Hector Horse and Felicity Filly kept arguing, arguing, and arguing about the children. Both wanted to keep them.

Chapter 2
Uncle Owen Makes a Decision

The three baby foals, Sena, Marnie, and Tisa, were very worried when they heard their parents arguing and fighting. They hated to hear the shouting, and they were scared that someone was going to get hurt. They hated to hear the bad names their parents called each other. It hurt their feelings! "You are a liar! You broke your promise!" shouted Hector Horse. "You are a thief! You are trying to steal my children!" yelled Felicity Filly. Sena, Marnie, and Tisa felt like crying. They loved both their parents and they wanted everyone to be a happy family.

Very soon the other farm animals in the neighborhood heard about the arguments, and they were all worried about the little foals. "It's not fair to the children to have their parents fighting over them like that!" clucked Mother Goose.

"I really don't know why Hector Horse and Felicity Filly call each other bad names!" said Bruce Bull, and he scratched his forehead with one large hoof.

"Hector Horse is really a fine, strong, kind, brown stallion and a very good father. Felicity Filly prances around a lot and likes to have fun, but she really loves those little foals," agreed Sally Sheep.

"Perhaps we could offer to help," suggested Candy Cow. We could call a big meeting of all the farm animals, and the wise old owl, Uncle Owen, can be the judge and decide who should look after the baby foals."

The next Monday morning, all the animals met together in a big circle. There were horses, cows, sheep, goats, chickens, ducks, geese, pigs, dogs, cats, and even two cute little yellow canaries. You can imagine all the mooing and grunting and squawking and baaing and tweeting! Uncle Owen Owl sat on a branch of the big oak tree overlooking everyone. "Order in the court!" he hooted, and everyone fell silent. "Let's hear Hector Horse tell his side of the story and Felicity Filly tell her side."

Hector Horse stood up. He looked very handsome with his brown coat brushed smooth. "I think I should have the children because I am older and more sensible than Felicity Filly. She is too young and silly. I will provide them with good food and teach them good values."

Felicity Filly stood up, her white silky coat shining in the sun, and she said, "I think I should have the children.

I am quite grown up now. I am not a teenager any longer. And I am not silly. I've learned a lot of important things these last few years from all my problems."

Uncle Owen Owl listened very carefully, and then he asked the other animals to give their opinions. They all told the owl judge that Hector Horse was a very good father and that Felicity Filly loved her children very much too.

"I have made a decision," said the wise old owl. "The little foals Tisa, Marnie, and Sena need both a mother and a father. They should spend some time with their father, and some time with their mother, and a big piece of time should be left for them to spend with their friends, to play, to go to school, and to learn. Felicity Filly should live in one barn on this side of town and Hector Horse can live in his own barn that he built on the other side of town. It is really better that they live apart and don't talk to each other much. They should be polite, however, if they should happen to meet on the same path."

All the animals cheered with moos and baas and bleats and grunts of approval when the wise old owl made that decision. Even Tisa, Marnie, and Sena felt a little bit better. They felt sad that their parents could not live together, but they hoped this would be the end of the fighting. They were relieved and even began to feel a little bit happier. "Would this be the end of their problems?" Sena wondered.

Chapter 3
Who Is Right and Who Is Wrong?

Sena, Marnie, and Tisa were growing up to be very pretty fillies. Each of them had brown coats like their Dad's and

"I have made a decision," said Uncle Owen. The little foals Tisa, Marnie, and Sena need both a mother and a father.

white silky patches on their foreheads and legs, just like their Mom's white silky coat. Sena had brown eyes like her Dad, and Marnie and Tisa had blue eyes like their Mom. Every day they played hide-and-seek together in the fields and ate lots of sweet green grass in the summertime and yellow hay in the wintertime. At the beginning of the week they lived with Felicity Filly in her barn on one side of town, and at the end of the week they lived with Hector Horse in his barn at the other side of town. In the middle of the week, they played with their friends and went to pony school.

Felicity Filly had to go to work, and she found a job as a circus pony at the fair. Each day she would dress up with pretty ribbons in her mane. She had her tail trimmed short. She painted her hoofs bright colors and wore a bright gold saddle and a bright gold bridle. At the circus, she would dance and prance and parade and perform gymnastic tricks, just as circus horses are supposed to do. Everyone clapped and cheered her because they thought she was pretty and cute and clever.

Now, Hector Horse had to work too. He worked on the farm, pulling the plow to till the land to grow hay, and dragging piles of wood together to make a new barn. On weekends, Saturday and Sunday, he took his little foals, Sena, Marnie, and Tisa, to the seaside to gallop along the beach and swim in the surf. Hector Horse wore a simple plain brown coat. He didn't like to fuss over his appearance.

Now, when Hector Horse saw Felicity Filly performing her gymnastic tricks at the fair, he was very scornful.

"Look at the stupid ribbon in her mane! Look at the silly colors she has painted on her hoofs. What a dumb job she has!" he said. "All she does is dance and prance and show off! I don't want my baby fillies to become like her! Felicity Filly doesn't use her brains!"

And when Felicity Filly saw Hector Horse on the farm, she scoffed, "Look at him out there in the dirty old field while my baby fillies are getting sunburned playing hide-and-seek. He doesn't polish and dress Marnie's coat, and Sena's hoofs are all cracked, and Tisa needs more exercise—she needs a gymnastics class to keep her fit!"

And so Felicity Filly and Hector Horse started arguing again. "You are dressing stupid, and you are teaching my baby foals to be stupid," shouted Hector Horse.

"I am not!" screamed Felicity Filly. "You are not taking good care of my baby foals!"

"They need me more because I am a sensible father and I teach them good values," Hector Horse declared.

"They need me more because I can teach them girl things and I have good values too," Felicity Filly answered.

Sena, Marnie, and Tisa looked at one another in dismay. Oh, dear, the fighting was starting all over again! And who was right and who was wrong? Was Felicity Filly right and Hector Horse wrong? Or was Hector Horse right and Felicity Filly wrong? Should they dress like Felicity Filly or should they dress like Hector Horse? Should they dance and prance at the circus, or should they work hard in the fields? Should they try to look pretty or should they try to use their brains?

Chapter 4
Sena, Marnie, and Tisa Find the Answer

Sena was very worried! She wanted to do the right thing. She wanted to grow up and have a happy life. Was Hector Horse right or was Felicity Filly right? Sena kept writing lists. On one side of the paper she wrote all the things her Dad said that were right, and she gave him one point for each. On the other side of the paper, she wrote all the things her Mom said that were right, and she gave her one point for each. Then she added up the points to see which one got the highest grade. Sometimes her Dad got the highest grade and sometimes her Mom got the highest grade. Then she worried that was not fair to her Dad so she gave him more points, so that he got the highest grade. She worried and worried and worried.

Marnie was different. She decided to tell Hector Horse and Felicity Filly each what they wanted to hear! At her Mom's barn, Marnie would say, "I love you best, Mommy. I want to live with you more. I want to have pretty ribbons in my mane just like you, Mommy. And I want to dance and prance like you!"

Then when Marnie went to her Dad's barn, she would say, "My Mommy is really silly. She wears this stupid ribbon in her mane. I love you best and I like living with you best, Daddy. I want to stay more with you."

Tisa, the littlest foal, told tales at both barns. She told her Dad that Felicity Filly kicked her, and sometimes she said that Felicity Filly left her for a long, long time with a pony sitter. When Hector Horse heard this, he got an-

grier with Felicity Filly. Then Tisa told her Mom that
Hector Horse said it was stupid to get exercise. Tisa also
told her Mom that her Dad said she could do whatever
she liked at her Mom's house, that she was the boss, not
her Mom, from now on. When Felicity Filly heard this,
she got angrier with Hector Horse.

The arguing between Hector Horse and Felicity Filly
got so bad that the three little foals decided to visit Uncle
Owen, the wise old owl judge, and get his advice. So they
set out one morning together and trotted down the road
to the old oak tree where Uncle Owen lived.

Uncle Owen was getting ready for his daytime nap,
but he was glad to see them. He invited them into his
tree trunk and served them some sweet pine nuts with
maple syrup, ice cream, and lemonade. Sena, Marnie, and
Tisa told him the long, long story and then asked him,
"Who is right and who is wrong? Is Hector Horse right
or is Felicity Filly right?"

Uncle Owen was silent for a long, long time, thinking and thinking. Then he hooted! "BOTH Felicity Filly
and Hector Horse are right! They BOTH have good
ideas about DIFFERENT things. It is important for you
to use your brains! It is also important for you to look
pretty and take care of your coats and your hoofs! It
is important to get exercise and to eat good healthy
foods! It is okay to prance and dance, but it is *also* important to work in the fields. At your Dad's barn, he is the
boss and you need to respect and obey him! At your
Mom's barn, she is the boss and you need to respect and
obey her!"

Now Tisa, Marnie, and Sena understood. They needed to choose good ideas from both their parents! And so as they grew up, they tried to use their brains at pony school, and also spent time choosing pretty bridles, saddles, and ribbons for their manes. And they kept their hoofs clean and their coats shining and ate lots of good foods and not too much candy. They grew up to be especially lovely young fillies because they became very wise and also full of fun. They learned different things from each parent.

But Sena, Marnie, and Tisa learned one MOST IM-PORTANT thing from BOTH their parents. They learned to be very caring, loving ponies because BOTH Hector Horse and Felicity Filly cared for them and loved them so very much!

CHAPTER 9

The Story of Jillaroo

JANET JOHNSTON

A common issue for divorced parents, especially for parents of very young children, is caretaking skills. Occasionally, one parent accuses the other of inadequate, neglectful, or even endangering caretaking. "The Story of Jillaroo" explores these issues and the toll on a child of being caught in the middle of very different parenting styles. The necessity for firm limits and rules as well as disengagement between the parents can provide safety for the child while building a relationship with each parent.

Chapter 1

Far, far away in the red-brown outback of Australia, among the scattered gums and the billabongs, lived many wild kangaroos. There were big ones and small ones, brown ones and gray ones, red ones and tan ones. Among the wildest and most beautiful of these animals was Naree. She had sleek, soft brown and gray fur with white markings on her forehead. Naree had boundless energy and enthusiasm for exploring the world. She climbed the high cliffs above the canyons, and she swam the deep waters in the gorges below. She nibbled grass along the creek beds where the crocodiles lay in wait, and she performed wonderful, weird hopping dances in the moonlight. She was quick and intelligent and resourceful.

Ranaroo was a great, handsome red kangaroo, the largest and finest of the species. He was intelligent but he was also calm and quiet. He liked to sit in the shade of the huge eucalyptus trees and think wonderful thoughts. He was a dreamer of wonderful dreams! He liked to watch the other kangaroos, but he did not like to join in the silliness of the other animals, as they hurried back and forth. One day as he was calmly watching and dreaming, he saw Naree dancing in a thunderstorm. As the lightning flashed around her, Naree danced a passionate dance, and Ranaroo, the great red kangaroo, was fascinated. He promised himself that one day Naree would be the mother of his child! And so he followed her and watched her every day, and he loved her, until she finally agreed to have a baby with him.

When Jillaroo, the baby kangaroo, was born, she was beautiful—like her mother she had the white markings on her forehead and her soft gray fur shone with red tinges in the sunlight, like her father's red coat. Naree loved the little joey that was living in her pouch, and Ranaroo was very proud of his family. He decided to go for a long trip over the mountains to look for a new billabong for Naree and Jillaroo.

One day as he was calmly watching and dreaming, he saw Naree dancing in a thunderstorm. As the lightning flashed around her, Naree danced a passionate dance, and Ranaroo, the great red kangaroo, was fascinated.

Now while he was gone, something terrible happened. Naree was hopping here and hopping there, living her usual busy life and having adventures with her baby Jillaroo tucked away in her pouch. One night she was bounding across a creek to reach the sweet grass on the other side when her baby bounced out of her pouch and hit her head on the rocks! Naree screamed with fright as she picked up her precious joey and saw all the blood covering her sweet little head. Quickly she called the other kangaroos for help, and they rushed Jillaroo to the medicine man. He was a wise old aboriginal who had many potent grasses and leaves that could help heal the little joey.

The aboriginals sent smoke signals across the mountains, conveying a message to Ranaroo, the father, to come home right away. Ranaroo was terribly worried when he heard the bad news. He hopped great long hops, faster and faster, all night and all the next day. And finally he arrived to be with little Jillaroo. Naree, the mother kangaroo, was terribly upset. It was the worst thing that could possibly have happened and she was frightened that her precious, beautiful little joey might die!

But Jillaroo was a strong little joey, and she slowly got better and the wound healed with just a little scar left on her forehead. She grew into a beautiful young kangaroo and began to spend more time hopping alongside her mother and father rather than living in Naree's pouch.

However, from that time on Naree and Ranaroo began to argue with each other. Ranaroo did not trust Naree to take care of his daughter, Jillaroo, and he said, "You were careless! You have no sense! You do stupid things! It is your fault that Jillaroo got hurt!" Naree was very upset "No! No! No! It was an accident! It was an accident!" She cried. Ranaroo said, "From now on *I* will take care of Jillaroo." Then Ranaroo decided to take Jillaroo with him on a long, long trip over the mountains, and he did not come back for a long, long time.

Now, Jillaroo was confused about what was happening. She liked to go on the long, long trip with Ranaroo, but she missed her mother, too. Sometimes she got scared and held on tightly to Ranaroo's paw. She no longer had her mother, and she was scared that she might also lose her father! Naree was very sad and missed her little joey very much. One day she set out to find her daughter. She bounded across the mountains and deserts until she reached the billabong where Ranaroo and little Jillaroo had set up camp. "I have come to see my daughter," Naree told Ranaroo.

Jillaroo was excited to see her mother, but she was also worried. She didn't quite trust that Naree would take care of her properly. She was most afraid that Naree might take her away and she wouldn't see Ranaroo again! She worried and worried and decided to be kind of mean to Naree. Sometimes, Jillaroo poked her tongue out at her mother, stamped her hind legs, and yelled a lot. Other times Jillaroo had such fun with Naree, dancing wild, weird dances in the moonlight and going on adventures together, that she forgot to be mean. And whenever Ranaroo and Naree argued and fought about who should be allowed to care of the young joey, Jillaroo held on tightly to Ranaroo's big red paw. The arguments got so bad that they decided to visit the chief of the aboriginal tribe and the wise old medicine man to help them solve the problem.

The chief of the aboriginal tribe and the wise old medicine man talked to everyone—they talked to Ranaroo, they talked to Naree, and they talked to Jillaroo. They also talked to the other animals—the wombats and the koala bears and the platypuses and the wallabies and the other kangaroos. Finally, they gave their advice. "Jillaroo needs both her mother and her father," the great chief said. "Jillaroo had a bad accident when she fell out of her mother's pouch. Naree is very, very sad about what happened, and she is trying to be an extra safe, good mother so that accidents will never happen again. Naree has lots of energy and good ideas; she will teach her daughter many things." The great chief then went on to say, "Jillaroo also needs to spend lots of time with her father. He is quiet and calm, and he soothes Jillaroo after she has had an exciting time with Naree. He can also take good care of her. Both Naree and Ranaroo are growing to be older, wiser kangaroo parents, and they both love their daughter very, very much! Jillaroo needs to spend time with both of her parents!

And that is exactly what happened. On some days, Jillaroo romped with her mother, she learned to jump long jumps, and she learned to read. On other days, Jillaroo sat under the eucalyptus tree with her father and listened to the music of the didgeridoo and shared in his dreams. She was fast growing up to be a beautiful, talented kangaroo because she had her mother's love for adventure and her father's quiet calmness. Furthermore, she was very intelligent like them both!

Chapter 2

The long, hot summer came to an end when the rains poured down in outback Australia. And still the animals ran to and fro, busy as usual. But Jillaroo and her father, Ranaroo, and her mother, Naree, no longer lived in that part of the country. They had hopped for many, many days and found a great new land with new mountains and valleys that were sometimes covered with snow. In this new land they met many new kinds of animals: there were lions and bears, dinosaurs and sharks living in this new country. There were also horses, cows, pigs, and chicken families.

In this new land, the big red kangaroo, Ranaroo, made a home together with a graceful deer called Dianadeer and a cute little Bambi-baby. All together they made a pretty nice family. Naree, the soft brown and gray kangaroo with white markings on her forehead, lived with her good friends the panda bear, a nice dinosaur, and several chickens. And what about Jillaroo? On some days she lived with Ranaroo and Dianadeer, where she loved to play with Bambi-baby. On other days she lived with Naree, where she especially liked to rough and tumble with Panda Bear. When she was with Naree, Jillaroo had lots and lots of things to do—she foraged for watercress and sweet grasses in the creek, she practiced her hopping and jumping, she had parties with the dinosaur and chickens, and she learned her ABC's and her times tables. Sometimes she got tired and a bit irritable when she was with Naree, because she was so busy. Then she was glad to sit down under the tree with Ranaroo and watch the sunset and the wind playing in the branches.

Unfortunately, Ranaroo and Naree continued to argue and fight with one another. Ranaroo still did not trust Naree to take good care of his daughter: "Don't go hopping around with her in your pouch so fast. . . . Wash behind her ears. . . . Don't be so busy. . . . Put ointment on the scar on her forehead. . . . Give her good food," and on and on. Naree's feelings were very hurt. She told Ranaroo: "I know how to take care of Jillaroo. I don't need you telling me what to do! I have better ideas than you. . . . You do not make Jillaroo practice her hopping and jumping. Jillaroo needs to learn more things!" And so they argued and argued!

The arguments sometimes were so bad that everyone got upset. All the other animals—the panda bear, the dinosaur, the chickens, and the deer—began to argue too. Everyone was irritable and snapped at one another. Even Ranaroo did not feel calm and quiet anymore. Some of the animals said that if this argument continued, they would just pack up and go and live somewhere else!

Jillaroo was sad and mad! She wished that Ranaroo and Naree could get along. She was worried that all of her wonderful friends—the panda bear, the dinosaur, the chickens, and the deer—might leave her and go away! Sometimes she wished she was not a kangaroo. She wished she could be a little bambi like Bambi-baby. If she was a bambi, she imagined she would live in just one place, with Ranaroo, where everyone liked one another. But then she knew deep inside that she would kind of miss the fun times they had together.

Jillaroo then felt like holding onto her mom real tight. Then she worried that if Ranaroo saw her nuzzle up to her mom, Ranaroo's feelings would be hurt and he might go away! Jillaroo was confused, but she did not want to talk about her sad and mad feelings to anybody. She tried very, very hard to be the best little kangaroo that she could be to make everyone happy again.

Ranaroo and Naree saw how hard Jillaroo was trying to be good. And they knew how sad and mad she was underneath. One day they looked at each other and said, "Enough! Enough! We have to stop the arguments! We have to make a plan about how to share little Jillaroo. We have to make up some rules about how to care for our beautiful little daughter. And we have to obey the rules!" And that is exactly what they did. With the help of the other animals, they wrote up some rules about the best way to care for a young kangaroo. They also decided to live in different valleys so there was less chance that they would meet on the same path and start arguing again. When they met together to make more plans and rules for Jillaroo, they had to practice being nice to each other. Sometimes they made mistakes and started arguing again, but then they remembered and tried to cooperate once more. Slowly, slowly, slowly everyone became calm again.

Most important of all, Jillaroo was happy and busy. She played with all her friends every day and she learned lots of exciting things about the world. She could dance, hop, and jump like her mother, and she dreamed wonderful dreams like her father. Most remarkably, she found that when she worked hard, she could make her dreams come true!

CHAPTER 10

Brenda Bear's Dream

JANET JOHNSTON

Some children, especially those older than nine or ten, tend to take sides when caught between parents in high-conflict divorce. These children tend to see one parent in a very positive way and the other as very undesirable. Visitation refusal may result with the rejected parent, forcing the child into a relationship against the child's wishes. An opportunity to experience both the strengths and the weaknesses of each parent is necessary for a child's own sense of individual identity to develop.

Brenda Bear was a pretty young brown bear who lived mostly with her father in a hollow tree in the mountains. On weekends and holidays she was supposed to visit her mother in a cave by the beach, but she didn't like going there very much. She got really tired and cross at the beach. Her mother *loved* to see her daughter when she came to visit, but then the mother bear made her practice fishing in the ocean all day long. She also had to chase seagulls along the beach all evening. Brenda would much rather have lazed in the sun with her father on top of the mountain. She also wanted to play with her friends, the opossums, on weekends or whenever she felt like it.

Although she could not remember her parents living together, Brenda Bear knew that many years ago, when she was a baby bear, her mother and father had lived in the same hollowed-out redwood tree. Unfortunately, now her parents did not get on very well. Brenda Bear felt very uncomfortable every time she went from the tree to the cave and back to the tree again, because these two big brown bears hissed, and spat and swatted each other. Brenda thought the arguments were her mother's fault. She thought the mother bear was always saying nasty things about her wonderful, big cuddly father bear. Brenda got angrier and angrier with her mother, and they started to hiss and spit and swat at each other, every time she went to visit.

Then something strange happened. Every night, when Brenda Bear nodded off to sleep after her bedtime story, she had the strangest dream. Brenda dreamed she lived in a weird, beautiful place where the sky was purple and the land was covered with beautiful flowers—pink, blue, yellow, red, and orange. In her dream Brenda Bear was ambling along a long winding white path through the fields of flowers and into a dark forest. She was traveling all by herself, but she was not lonely and she was not scared. She was excited because she was going to visit the castle on the other side of the woods where the Good Fairy Queen lived. She hoped that the Good Fairy Queen would wave her magic wand and make her into a princess. Brenda Bear trotted along faster and faster and finally came to the castle and banged on the big gate!

"Come in! Come in !" said the Good Fairy Queen. "I am so glad to see you, my beautiful little Brenda Bear." The Good Fairy Queen had a warm welcoming smile on her face. She looked very lovely in her flowing pink dress. "Come, my little one, come and eat all these wonderful cakes and cookies I prepared for you!" Brenda Bear ate hungrily and soon she was filled and couldn't eat anymore. "Come my little one, have some more, have some more," the Good Fairy Queen said. "No thank you. I want you to make me into a princess now," Brenda Bear replied.

"No! No! You must eat all the cakes I have made you first!" the Good Fairy Queen insisted. Now Brenda Bear was getting pretty angry and she yelled at the Good Fairy Queen, "You are not listening to me! I have had enough to eat! Make me into a princess RIGHT NOW!" It was then that the strangest thing happened.

Right in front of her very eyes, the Good Fairy Queen turned into an ugly wicked witch with a mean green face. "Eat! Eat! Eat!" she screeched in her harsh voice. Now, Brenda Bear wasn't really frightened of the wicked old witch—but she was really, really mad.

"No, you ugly fleabag!" she yelled. "I am not going to do anything you say! I am going to tell the good wizard on you!" and she galloped out the castle gate really fast.

As Brenda Bear bounded over the creek, she caught

Right in front of her very eyes, the Good Fairy Queen turned into an ugly wicked witch with a mean green face. "Eat! Eat! Eat!" she screeched in her harsh voice.

sight of her reflection in the water, and to her surprise, she didn't see her pretty little brown furry face. Instead, she saw an ugly black twisted little face with a mean look in its eyes. "That's weird," she thought to herself and sat down on her back legs to look more closely in the water. "What's happened to my pretty face?" she cried, and she began to sob.

Just then, Brenda Bear saw another reflection in the water beside her. It was the ugly wicked witch who had followed her. But something strange happened again. The ugly wicked witch changed back into the Good Fairy Queen, who picked her up in her arms and gave her a cuddle and a kiss. "I am sorry," said the Good Fairy Queen. "I didn't mean to upset you. I just had a bad day. Let's make up and be good friends again." And so they did! Then when Brenda Bear looked back down in the water, she discovered that her ugly black twisted little face with a mean look had gone and she was a pretty little bear again.

Right then, Brenda Bear woke up from her dream. What a weird dream I had, she thought. I wonder what it means.

CHAPTER 11

In a Kingdom by the Sea

KAREN BREUNIG

Some children carry a heavy burden when their parents divorce. As if coping with their own feelings is not enough, many children struggle with the feelings each parent expresses, sometimes even believing that their parents' feelings of sadness or anger are their responsibility. They may feel like the court jester in this story, hiding their own feelings in the interest of making each parent feel better. "In a Kingdom by the Sea" relieves children of this burden, reassuring them that parents are responsible for their own feelings and their own healing following a divorce.

Once upon a time, many years ago, in a kingdom by the sea lived a king and queen. Their castle was built high on a hill, overlooking a beautiful valley that opened up to the sea. They could see for miles from their window. They could even see ships sailing way out on the ocean.

89

One ordinary day, just like any other, the king called for the royal court jester. This jester had been with the king and queen for many years. It was his job to keep the king and queen happy, to make them smile when they were sad, and to tell amusing stories to take away their worries.

Some days, he worked so hard he had no time to practice his juggling and singing. He hoped someday to be the best juggler and singer in the land, but more and more he had to spend his time making the royal couple smile.

Now, on this particular day the king looked very sad. "I'm feeling awful today, oh loyal jester," said the king. "Oh boy," thought the jester, "Do I ever have a lot of work to do to make this sad face smile again."

The king went on to explain that he was very confused about his queen. Long ago, when he and the queen married, she seemed to him to be perfect in every way. He felt then that he would be happy with her for the rest of his life. Now, he explained, he was starting to think that maybe she wasn't so perfect. She had opinions about everything, it seemed—about how to run the kingdom, what to pay the workers, how often to invite the royal relatives over for dinner. And she sometimes disagreed with the king. "I wish," said the king, "that I could have that beautiful young woman again that I married. We loved each other so much back then. We never argued." The king looked at the jester. His face turned from sad to mad. "I command you to make us happy again," he shouted. "I command you to make all of these worries go away. You have a week to figure something out. Now, get to it!"

Later that afternoon, the queen approached the jester

as he sat under the willow tree practicing his juggling. "Stop what you are doing," the queen said abruptly. "You must help me, jester. I am so confused." "Uh-oh, here it comes," he thought. "I'm going to be busy for the rest of my life keeping these people happy." But he listened respectfully, for he thought this was his job.

The queen went on, "My husband, the king, seems to be getting grumpier as the years pass. He is no longer that energetic, lighthearted man I married so long ago. I am so confused, because I loved that young man so very much. Where did he go? Now all we do is argue. We can't seem to agree on anything.

"What can I do, loyal jester? Could you perhaps dance in some magic way and make us happy again? You have to think of something! You above all others have the power to make us laugh." The queen paused thoughtfully, gazing out at the far-off ocean. Then she turned quickly to the jester and shouted, "I command you to make us happy again. You have one week. Now, get to it!"

The jester walked slowly back to his royal apartment. His head hung low, his heart was heavy, and he was scared. "What will happen to me if I can't make the king and queen happy again, if I can't keep them together? Where will I go, what will I do? Will they throw me out of the royal castle? Who will care about me?" So many questions tumbled around in his head that his brain got very tired. All he wanted to do was sleep. He fell on his bed and pulled the covers up over his head. Soon he was dreaming.

He dreamed that night of a big storm that came off the sea. The winds were high and the rain fell in buckets. The whole valley was flooded. It was his job to save all the people of the village, but try as he might, he couldn't get to them because he didn't have a boat. He awoke the next morning in a terrible mood.

The rest of the week didn't go much better. The jester worked furiously, learning new tricks and new jokes that he hoped would make the royal couple happy again. He practiced some new dance steps he had seen the villagers do. He learned some new stories from the traveling minstrel. And every night he dreamed of the big storm.

A week went by and the king and queen called him into the royal living room. They were both looking pretty glum. They had just had an argument about what to have for dinner.

The jester began with the jokes. Nobody laughed. He then moved onto the stories. The royal couple yawned. He next tried the magic tricks. They applauded politely when he was done, but no one smiled. So he tried the new dance steps. He was beginning to get very nervous. He tripped over his own feet and felt tears well up in his eyes. He had done absolutely the best he could but still the royal couple frowned and glared at each other. The king called out, "That will be all, jester. This is not helping. You may leave."

The jester returned to his room, lay down on his bed, and cried. He felt that this was all his fault. "If I had only been a better jester, I would have been able to make them happy," he thought. He didn't sleep well that night. When he awoke, he overheard the maids talking about the king and queen. It had been announced that the king would move out immediately and take over the castle that sat on a hill at the opposite end of the valley. He would take some of the royal helpers with him; others would remain with the queen. The jester worried, what would become of him, where would he live, what would his job be?

From that day on life was very different for the jester. He had to divide himself between the king's castle and the queen's castle. Keeping the queen happy in her castle and the king happy in his castle took up all his time. And keeping track of the schedule made his head spin. "Let's see, if today is Monday, I'm with the king. No, that's not right. It's the king on Tuesday and the queen on Monday. No, that's only if I've just spent the weekend with the king! Aaaugh!!! I'm never going to get used to this."

And that wasn't the worst of it. The king was always asking the jester what was going on at the queen's castle. And at least once a day the queen would ask the jester who was his favorite, and whose castle he liked better. Both the king and the queen said mean things about each other in front of the jester. They would ask him to agree with them. The jester didn't know how to answer these questions. They made him squirm. He felt as if he was not being loyal to the queen if he reported her activities to the king. And he knew the queen wanted him to say he liked her castle the best, but if he said that, he would feel disloyal to the king. So he just kept quiet, which only made the king and queen try harder to get him to talk. Sometimes he felt like a ball being tossed back and forth.

It was getting harder and harder to do his job. It seemed that both the king and the queen were always unhappy, and try as he would, nothing he did helped. He felt like a failure. "Some jester you are," he would say to himself. "You can't seem to make anyone smile anymore."

He was lost in his thoughts one day as he walked quickly through the village on his way to the king's castle. He often walked this way, through the village gate and past the old stone well. This particular day an old woman was sitting by the well. She smiled at the jester. "Good morning," she said. "Could you lend me a hand with this bucket? My old hands just don't work like they used to." "Sure," the jester said distractedly. He helped her lift the heavy bucket filled with water and pour it into her jug.

She said "thank you," with a twinkle in her eye and a mysterious smile. "You seem to have misplaced your spirit this morning, young man," she said. The jester looked at her puzzled. "What's that you mean, old woman?" he said. She winked at him. "Why, I've been around long enough to recognize a troubled heart when I see one. What is it, son, that lays so heavy on your heart?" The jester looked into her kindly face. He told her that he thought he was a failure as a jester. He told her how hard his job had become now that the king and queen lived apart. "Try as I might, I just can't seem to make them happy anymore. I'm useless. My jokes don't work. My magic tricks fall flat." A tear came to his eye.

It was quiet for a minute. The old woman's eyes softened as she looked at him. "You are trying to do a job that is impossible," she said. "You cannot make another person smile if there is no happiness in him already. He is responsible for that happiness, not you. It would be like trying to fetch water from an empty well. It is not in your power to fill an empty well. What you are responsible for is yourself and your own happiness." She paused.

The jester sat down by the well and thought of what the old woman had said. "But it makes me feel good to make others happy," he replied. "That's been my job for a long time. What would I do if I didn't do that?"

"What do you enjoy doing just for yourself?" she asked.

At first, he couldn't remember anything. Then it started to come back to him. He had once dreamed of being the best juggler and singer in the land. He loved the feel of balls flying through the air, his hands moving swiftly and skillfully. And to fill the air with song made his heart light and joyful. "Why, it's juggling and singing that I love the most," he told the old woman. "I once thought that I might one day be the best in the land, but I have had so much work to do with the king and queen that I gave up my singing and juggling." "Perhaps it is time to try them again." The old woman smiled slightly as she spoke.

"Perhaps it is time for you to stop trying to get water from an empty well. Perhaps it is time for you to reach down into your own well. You may find there's abundant water there to quench your thirst."

She tapped her cane on the ground. "And now," she said, "would you happen to have any balls with you? It would be lovely to see you juggle." The jester dug his balls out from the bottom of his pack. They hadn't been used in months. He began slowly but soon he remembered the feel of it. Before long he was juggling three, four, even five balls. And he was smiling to himself.

He began slowly but soon he remembered the feel of it. Before long he was juggling three, four, even five balls. And he was smiling to himself.

When he was done, he looked down to thank the old woman for her kindness, but there was no one there. He was standing alone in the village square smiling to himself, scratching his head.

From that day forward things started to change. The jester began to worry less about the king and queen. And he started to think a little bit more about juggling and singing. In fact, he decided he didn't want to be a jester anymore. He was tired of having to keep everyone happy. He found himself a school where he could take singing and juggling lessons and he enrolled. Now, he still cared about the king and queen. And he still visited them often. But he didn't feel responsible for them. And when they would start to talk about each other, he would ask them not to do that in front of him; he said it made him feel uncomfortable. Then he would go off to practice his singing and juggling.

He practiced so much and for so long that he became known as the best singer and juggler in the land. He traveled all over doing what he loved. It made his heart happy. And it just so happened that it made others, even the king and queen, smile to hear him and see his juggling.

He never did run into that old woman again, though he looked for her in many a village. But he thought of her whenever he saw a well. And he smiled to himself.

PART III

Severe Divorce Concerns

CHAPTER 12

Good Time Recipes

CARLA GARRITY

Some children refuse visitation with a parent because of a serious problem that parent has not resolved. Time spent together may be unpleasant and even frightening because of a parent's unpredictable behavior or verbal outbursts. Learning ways to feel safe, to cope, and to minimize exposure to that parent's personal difficulties is essential for a child to be able to visit and build a relationship.

Once upon a time a most unusual thing happened. One large porcupine and one medium-sized beaver not only found themselves together but also became a mom and dad to three babies. This is not going to be a happy story because papa porcupine and mama beaver did not laugh and have fun together. They liked to do things in very different ways, and they would argue and fuss. So how did this "not so happy story" happen?

It all began when the bulldozers, tractors, and other big machines came to the meadow where many animal families lived. The big machines started digging and plowing to make way for new homes for people. Bluejay, who flew around and knew about the world, warned the animals to find a new home. He had seen before what happened when the big machines came. Porcupine and Beaver did not take heed though—Porcupine because he was rather old, stubborn, set in his ways, and not interested in finding a new home. Beaver did not listen either; she was certain Bluejay was exaggerating. She would find a new place to live nearby and be just fine. She had always managed to make do in a pinch and she would do it again. So Porcupine and Beaver, who did not even know each other before this story began, both were hiding and sleeping when the machines came.

One day the noises stopped and they crawled out of their hiding places. Neither one could believe what they saw. The trees were gone, the wonderful underbrush where they stayed on hot days, the grasses, the flowers, and most all of their meadow was gone. There was dirt everywhere, piles of dirt and sand and big, big holes in the ground.

Being a hard worker, as well as a worrier, Beaver immediately began to be concerned about a place to live and enough food to survive. She scurried around the dirt piles looking to see whether any place was left for a home. Luckily she found a mulberry tree with some small berries and a large tree stump that had not been destroyed. She ran to share her good news with Porcupine, who had curled up to take a nap while Beaver was gone. Sleepily he followed her to the log and, once inside, resumed his nap.

Months went by and in spite of many long walks looking for their old friends, Porcupine and Beaver never ran across another animal. Spending all their time together, they grew a bit fond of each other but they never really learned to get along. Beaver was always annoyed with Porcupine, who slept most of the time and rarely looked for food. Porcupine, on the other hand, was weary just watching Beaver scurrying around to make their log nicer with what dried leaves she could find. He wished she would be quieter, as he was, and rest sometimes. Still they enjoyed each other's company in the evening when it grew dark and especially when winter came and it grew cold. Together they would chat about how life had been before the big machines.

When spring arrived, so did their new family. Three little babies were born to Beaver. All three were light golden brown with soft, soft fur. Beaver loved to sleep with her babies curled up beside her, nursing and caring for them. At first, Porcupine was happy, too, for Beaver was quieter and not scurrying here and there all the time. She stayed in the log, nursing and tending their babies. But the babies grew and they no longer stayed still and quiet. They were even noisier and busier than their mother, and Porcupine became grumpy indeed. Their log home was filled with commotion all day long and even during the nights sometimes. No longer could he curl up in his corner for a nice afternoon nap. He grew grumpier and grumpier.

One day he became so grumpy when his nap was in-

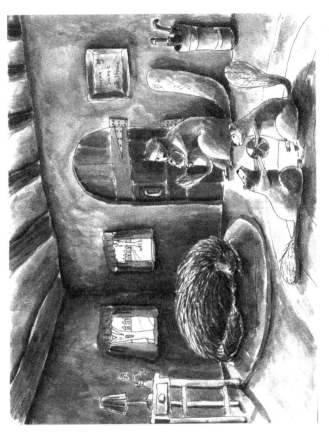

But the babies grew and they no longer stayed still and quiet. They were even noisier and busier than their mother, and Porcupine became grumpy indeed.

terrupted that he shot some quills across the log. One quill barely missed his little son, who cried and shook as he realized how much it would hurt to have been hit by a flying quill. Beaver was scared too, and she suggested to her three children that they had all best leave Papa Porcupine alone to have his nap. Actually, Mama Beaver knew it was time to find a new log for herself and her children. She knew that the children would become ever louder and more rambunctious as they grew older, and that Porcupine would probably shoot his quills again.

They walked and walked, running quickly between the houses that had now been built. Some things were beginning to form again: new trees at the stumps of old ones, little shrubs and small flowers. Finding a new home would not be so difficult after all, and soon she found just the right spot. A little growth of new trees was sprouting where five large trunks had fallen. Together they formed shelter, but best of all they also made a playground. One trunk had fallen on another so that it was perfect to run up and jump into a soft bed of leaves and little twigs. The children adored it and played and played all afternoon while Beaver finally had a nap of her own.

The next morning, Mama Beaver and the children hurried through the meadow to their old log home to tell Porcupine where they would be living. He grunted and snorted that finally he would have some peace and quiet, but that it would be pleasant to have his children visit from time to time. He thought he was too old and weary to walk to their new home, and Beaver agreed that she would walk the children part of the way and let them make the rest of the journey on their own, now that they were a bit older. This would give her a chance to look for food while they were visiting.

The first few visits seemed to be fine, but then one day, Mama Beaver met the children for the walk back home and found all of them chattering so quickly that she could barely understand what they were saying. She had to help them take turns by deciding who would speak first. Becky began by saying that Porcupine was too old and boring to visit; she did not want to go anymore. She would help her mother find food—that would be more fun. Danny was even more upset. He had tried to curl up next to Porcupine to have a nap too and found all the quills pokey and sticky. "No one can be cozy next to a prickly old thing like he is," Danny said angrily, then he recalled the day of the flying quills and before he could finish, his brother Ned burst into tears and yelled that he had been hit with four quills when he asked Papa Porcupine for a snack. "He's no fun, he's too old, he's too prickly," they all began to chant together.

Mama Beaver understood how her children felt; she, too, had found Porcupine prickly to sleep by and boring sometimes and even scary when he was irritated. Mother also was a smart beaver, and she knew some tricks for getting along with Porcupine. She called them her recipes for a good time:

1. Wait until Porcupine is asleep to curl up next to him. He folds his quills neatly by his side when he is sleeping, and then he is much softer to sleep next to.

2. Hunt for food on the walk over and have a picnic when you get there. Papa Porcupine does like to have picnics, but he doesn't like to go out looking for food.

3. Quiet moments are nice too. Porcupine likes to play thinking games like leaf checkers and twenty forest questions. He especially likes reading animal stories and talking about the meadow when he was younger.

4. A short visit is best. Porcupine gets cranky after too much time. He snorts and shuffles around and wants to take a nap. That is how you can tell his cranky moods are beginning. That is the time to say "good-bye" and to remind him that you will see him again in a few days.

Mama's recipes helped. They did not work all the time, but they worked most of the time, and as Danny, Ned, and Becky grew older, they learned how to create recipes of their own.

CHAPTER 13

Elephant Island

KAREN BREUNIG

Divorce often results in angry, rageful feelings in the adults. Sometimes this anger was present prior to the divorce and has impacted the child's relationship with one or both parents. "Elephant Island" is a story for children struggling to cope with the fear a parent's anger engenders. Concrete suggestions for coping with a parent's angry outbursts are offered to ease the fears present during visitation.

Chapter 1

Once upon a time, long ago, on a beautiful island in the middle of a blue-green sea lived two young elephants, Tony and Sally. They were not alone on this island but

---

"Elephant Island" was written in consultation with Carla Garrity and Mitchell Baris.

109

lived with their mother and the rest of their tribe, which included old elephants, young elephants, and those in between. They were the youngest of the elephants, and they were well loved by their mother and the other members of the tribe.

The tribe lived in a beautiful, sunny meadow near the white sand beach. Most of their days were spent doing those things that young elephants love to do. The played on the white sand and splashed in the green sea. They sprayed themselves to keep cool on hot summer days. And they loved to explore the lush, moist jungle that bordered their meadow. They were like most young creatures in this world. They were curious about everything. There was so much to see and so much to learn on their island. Exploring and learning about their world took up much of their time.

One part of the island they had not yet explored. It was the far side, north of where the tribe lived. There was a volcano there. They could see it from the meadow, poking its head out of the dark, rich jungle. Sometimes they could see steam escape from its top. Sometimes they felt a slight rumble of the earth beneath their feet. Grandpa Elephant explained to them, "The volcano is part of your home. It is because of the volcano that this island is here. It is the volcano's hot rocks and lava that have slowly, over many years, built up the rich earth on which our jungle grows. And that earth gives us sweet fruits and fragrant flowers." Grandpa went on, "But you must be aware of the dangers."

They were curious about the volcano and the other side of the island, but it also scared them. It seemed you could never tell when the volcano would explode. Sometimes they wished the volcano would just disappear. But their Mom said the volcano was a part of their home and they would have to learn how to live safely with it, because it wasn't going away. Now that they were bigger, they liked to wander farther and farther from their Mom to explore the far reaches of their jungle home. Mom would not always be with them to warn them about the volcano's eruptions. So it was very important that they learn about the volcano themselves.

One day Grandpa, Mom, Tony, and Sally set off through the jungle in the direction of the volcano. The jungle they passed through was at first very familiar to Sally and Tony. They had explored much of it before. It was full of exotic flowers and luscious fruit. The air was moist and warm. Bright, colorful birds fluttered from treetop to treetop. They came eventually to a place that was not familiar to them. It was here that Grandpa turned to Mom and said, "It's time for you and me to turn back and let these young elephants go on by themselves." Mom was a little uneasy. She asked Grandpa, "Aren't they a little young to be exploring by themselves?" He just smiled and shook his head "No." She handed them a basket filled with their favorite foods and other things and told them she loved them very much. She hesitated and then said she knew they would learn much more about the volcano if they explored it themselves. Mom had heard that a rare and delicious fruit was found only on the sides of the volcano. She reminded them to keep their eyes open for it.

After Mom and Grandpa left, Sally and Tony sat down

on the dark, moist floor of the jungle and thought about what they should do. Sally felt responsible for Tony since she was older. She thought maybe it was her job to figure out the volcano and then explain it to Tony. That made her worry since she wasn't sure she was going to be able to understand what made a volcano erupt any better than Tony could. The more she worried, the more her stomach hurt. She decided to think about what was right in front of her. That seemed to help her when she got scared. She thought about the basket her Mom had given them and what wonderful foods might be inside. She let her mind get busy thinking about making lunch.

Tony, meanwhile, was thinking about his Mom and being back in the meadow with the rest of the tribe. The more he thought about it, the sadder he got. Tears started to fill his eyes. He stood up and started to head back in the direction of the meadow, when he felt a deep rumbling beneath his feet. The earth seemed to sway back and forth. He heard a loud boom and looked in the direction of the volcano. Steam and red-hot rocks were flying from the top of the volcano. Tony fell to his knees and hid his face in the grass and waited for the noises to stop. He was shaking with fear. Small, hot rocks were falling around him. One landed right on his head. "Ouch!" he cried. He felt his head. He was bleeding. He looked over and saw Sally covering her eyes too. He called to her and she dug a bandage out of their basket and covered his cut with it. He wished harder than ever that he was home. And he wished that the eruption would just stop. Finally it did. The jungle was very quiet. "Was it safe again?" Tony worried.

Chapter Two

Just then Sally and Tony heard a rustling of leaves off to the side. Out from under a beautiful green bush with small purple flowers came the strangest little creature they had ever seen. It seemed to be a skinny monkey with a tail twice as long as her body. Her brown fur was about two inches long all around, and it stuck straight out. She had eyes the color of a jungle pool and a nose as dark as a moonless night. There was fur all around her mouth, but when she spoke they could catch little glimpses of a pink tongue.

At first, Sally and Tony weren't sure whether to be frightened or not. The monkey stood there and smiled at them. They glanced at each other then burst into peals of laughter. They were so relieved to meet a friendly creature here at the foot of the volcano. Perhaps this monkey knew something about volcanoes, something she was willing to teach them. They waited for her to speak.

"My name is Smiley," she said. "You two seem to be lost. I thought maybe I could be of some help. What are your names?" Sally spoke first. "Well, I'm Sally and this here is Tony. He's my younger brother. We came here to learn about volcanoes. Our Mom says it's important that we learn all about our island, about the good things and the scary things too, so that we can be safe and know how to take care of ourselves even when she's not around. But I don't know about this erupting stuff. It's really scary. I wish the volcano would just go away, or maybe never erupt anymore."

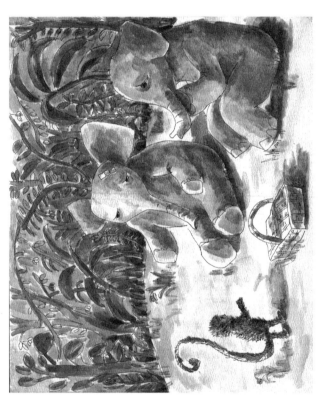

Out from under a beautiful green bush with small purple flowers came the strangest little creature they had ever seen. It seemed to be a skinny monkey with a tail twice as long as her body. Her brown fur was about two inches long all around, and it stuck straight out.

Tony spoke up. "Yeah, I just want this all to go away. I want to be back with my Mom. I don't understand why I have to know anything about volcanoes anyway." Tony sounded angry.

Smiley was listening very carefully. "Things that scare us often make us angry, too," she said. "And this volcano can sure be scary at times."

"Now, about volcanoes and eruptions. Well, I know some things about them. I lived here in this jungle all my life. And my parents and grandparents and great-grand-parents before me. We've had to learn to live with this volcano. Maybe the things I know will help you. But first, how about lunch? I'm hungry and it looks as if you've got some good stuff in that basket of yours. Let's eat!"

So Sally and Tony spread out the blanket Mom put in the basket and sat down with their new friend on the jungle floor. Mom remembered to pack all their favorite foods—including a big bunch of bananas. Smiley's eyes twinkled when she saw the bananas. "Why, your Mom must have known you'd run into a monkey!"

Between bites, Smiley looked up and said, "Well, what is it you'd like to know about volcanoes?" Sally was busy fixing a sandwich for Tony. She noticed her stomach was starting to hurt. Maybe just from being hungry, she thought. Or maybe from missing Mom. Sometimes she wished she was still a baby elephant. They stay by their Mom's side waking and sleeping. But baby elephants don't get to explore the jungle and splash in the sea with their friends. They're safe with their moms, but they don't yet know how to take care of themselves. They can't go off on adventures alone or with their friends. Or even with their brothers.

Brothers! They could be fun or they could be big pests. Sally wished that sometimes Tony would make his own sandwich. When would he be big enough to take care of himself? Her stomach was hurting from being hungry, but she still made his lunch first. Maybe next time she'd teach him how to make his own sandwich. He was a smart elephant, after all. Then she could make her own when she was hungry. Maybe her stomach wouldn't get so tied up in a knot waiting for food.

"Well, what I'd like to know is why these volcanoes blow their tops anyway," said Tony. "Why couldn't our island have a regular, ordinary mountain that sits peacefully with its head in the clouds?"

"I don't think I can answer that," said Smiley. "None of the monkeys who came before me ever understood why our island got a mountain that blew its top and other islands didn't. It just seems to be the way things are. They decided to try to figure out how to live with this volcano instead of spending a lot of time wondering why it was here in the first place. One thing they did notice is that the lava and ash from the volcano seem to make the soil rich."

Smiley went on, "And why volcanoes blow their tops? Well, I think it's that they have lots of hot rock, steam, and fire in their center. The fire and hot melted rock makes so much steam that it has to find a place to come out. It pushes its way up through cracks and openings in the volcano. Then BOOM, it flies up through the air and the lava pours down the sides. If you're too close when it erupts, you can get hurt. I know, I've had my fur singed more than a few times. What makes it erupt at some times and not at others is a question all the monkeys before me spent a lot of time trying to answer. They came up with a few ideas that I'll tell you about later."

Tony wasn't sure whether he could believe this funny little monkey. He watched her very carefully, trying to figure out what she was all about. She got up and put her ear to the ground. She stayed that way for what seemed like a long time. Then she climbed up very high in a nearby tree and sat there quietly listening. "Sometimes," she said, "you can hear the sounds of the volcano in the earth before you hear it in the air. And sometimes, you can hear changes in the sounds of the jungle animals. They seem to chatter more; the birds squawk louder. I pay attention to these things."

Smiley went on, "Some days this volcano doesn't erupt at all. Some days it erupts many times. Sometimes they are just small eruptions; sometimes they are large and very scary. If I am close to the volcano and feel rumblings of the earth or hear any hissing sounds, I find shelter right away. There are caves all over the sides of this volcano. I get to one of them. I stay inside my cave and listen very carefully to the noises from the volcano. I have lots of things I do inside my cave to keep myself busy while I wait for the volcano to be silent. I do somersaults and stand on my head. I practice standing on my toes and stretching up as far as I can. Some of the caves have bars for me to swing from. We monkeys love to swing! There are times when I play tic-tac-toe in the dirt or collect rocks and sticks and build a village. Sometimes I make up stories; sometimes I write them down. Lots of times I pretend I'm somewhere else, like at the beach, and I think about what I would be doing if I were there. Sometimes I draw pictures of me at the beach or in my cave being safe. Sometimes I sing a song inside my head. I don't let the volcano hear my song. All these things help me to forget a little about just how loud and scary the volcano can be.

"Well, enough talking. Let's go find these caves. You two will have to start learning where the caves are if you expect to be able to explore this volcano and be safe." Smiley jumped up and started to pack the rest of their lunch. Tony folded the blanket and tucked it back in the basket. He was feeling a little less scared now that his tummy was full. And he was getting more and more curious about this funny little monkey and what she had to show them.

Chapter 3

Off Smiley scampered down a path that led into the dark and unfamiliar jungle. Sally followed, with Tony close behind. Smiley reminded them to keep their eyes open for the luscious, rare fruit that grows only on the sides of the volcano. "This must be the same fruit Mom was talking about," thought Sally.

"What color is it?" asked Tony.

"Why, it can be many colors," said Smiley. "I've seen it red and yellow and green, even blue one time. Once you taste how delicious it is, you will never forget it. Sometimes it grows on bushes down low and it can be hidden from view by the leaves. It is also known to grow on tall, graceful trees. Sometimes you can reach it by just standing on your tippy toes. Then there are times it is just out of your reach and it can be very frustrating. That has even happened to me, a monkey, that I could see the fruit but could not get to it. I was very disappointed, then very angry, then very sad, all at the same time!"

Smiley jumped up and, grabbing a long vine, swung high into the branches of a banana tree. From there she reached out to the next tree, and the next, and the next. She moved through the jungle so quickly and gracefully. She looked back frequently to make sure she hadn't left her friends behind. "We'll be at the first cave soon," she said. "It's just around that ridge over there."

Tony was glad to hear they were almost there. He was getting tired and he was beginning to think about his Mom and the tribe again. "I think after we see this cave I'm going to go back to the meadow," he announced in a loud voice. Just then the ground began to rumble. Smiley hurried them into the cave. They heard hissing sounds then the rumblings died down. "Doesn't sound like it's going to amount to much," said Smiley, "but we'd better stay in here for a few minutes to be safe.

"Funny thing about this volcano. Some of the monkeys say the volcano gets lonely and loves to have visitors. But its huffing and puffing and blowing its top scares the visitors. It seems it doesn't understand just how scary it is."

Smiley paused a minute. She put her ear to the opening of the cave. She listened to the sounds of the jungle. The volcano seemed to have died down.

She continued, "We monkeys visit the volcano once a week. Sometimes if I'm scared I get busy with roller-skating or play ball or make up games. I do a lot of exploring, too. That's how I found the caves. I searched for that rare fruit, as well. It was always a special day when I found one. The sweetness of that fruit seemed to make it a little easier to put up with the eruptions. But I always listen for the sounds of an eruption so I can get to a cave. I'm safe in a cave."

Smiley gave the thumbs up sign. The volcano was quiet. It was time to go. She jumped up and led the way out of the cave. Sally followed. Tony didn't move. Tony wasn't so sure he wanted to leave the cave. It felt pretty safe in there. "Come on," urged Sally, "Let's go. Do you need me to help you up?" Sally often felt as if it was her job to get him to go places and do things. That could be really hard sometimes, especially when Tony didn't want to go. He could be very stubborn.

Smiley went over and put her arm around Sally. She whispered quietly in Sally's ear, "You must get tired of trying to be in charge of Tony. Maybe it's time you let someone else help him. That someone can be me!" Sally's eyes started to fill with tears. For the first time she realized that it was a hard job, and sometimes a scary job. She was tired. It made her anxious at times. What if she told Tony the wrong things to do or couldn't get Tony to do what others wanted him to do? She could have everyone mad at her. It might be nice to let someone else do this job. She loved Tony a lot. That wouldn't change. But her life would seem easier if she were just in charge of herself. She smiled at Smiley and nodded her head. Smiley nodded back and walked over to where Tony was sitting. Smiley talked quietly with him and pretty soon he was up and ready to go. Sally felt a little lighter. "This Smiley sure is beginning to feel like a friend," she thought.

Chapter 4

"Now I'm going to show you one of my favorite places on this part of the island," said Smiley. They followed Smiley up a ridge and down a little slope that was covered with delicate yellow blossoms. "Wow, this sure smells good!" yelled Sally. At the bottom of the hill was a small stream. They stopped for a drink, then followed the stream down the slope for what seemed like a long time. The jungle was filled with a fine mist of water. The smell was rich and dark. The splashing and gurgling of the stream was a friendly sound. It got louder and louder. They came at last to a beautiful waterfall. Smiley jumped right under the spray and spun around a few times. She giggled and danced and beckoned for Tony and Sally to join her. Tony jumped right in, splashing his big feet up and down. Sally filled her trunk up with cool water and sprayed it all over her back. She joined the dance too, swinging her trunk back and forth to make bigger and bigger splashes in the water.

"So there are some fun places on this volcano after all," said Tony.

"And another cave is right over there," said Smiley. She pointed to a rocky outcrop just about ten yards away. "This is where we're going to spend the night."

"Spend the night!" shouted Tony. "No way!" Just then the rumblings started again. They could feel them in their bodies and hear them over the sound of the waterfall. Sally moved quickly in the direction of the cave without stopping much to think. Tony wasn't sure, at first, just what was happening. He looked up toward the mouth of the volcano and saw hot red rocks flying through the air. Then he understood. It was another eruption. He heard Smiley calling to him. "Get to the cave." Just as he made it through the opening, he heard a BOOM. Rocks were falling right where he had been standing a few seconds ago!

Tony let out a big sigh of relief. He sat down next to Smiley as she began to open the basket. She spread Mom's blanket out to cover the floor of the cave. "Pretty cozy in here, if I do say so myself!" she said. "Not a bad place to spend the night. Then tomorrow morning it will be time for you two to return to the meadow. You've both learned a lot about this part of the island in a short time. On your next visit I'll be here to help you. There will be lots more things to learn and lots more jungle to explore. After all, this is part of your home, too. The more you learn about how to take care of yourselves here, the more it will feel like home."

Smiley found some ripe bananas and began to eat. The eruption continued outside. Sally decided to ignore it for now. She turned to Tony. "Tony, let me show you how to make your sandwich." Tony moved over closer to Sally. He tried hard to pay attention to what she was showing him. The more he paid attention to what she was doing, the less he noticed the booming outside. He did like the idea of being grown up enough to make his own sandwich. "I'm not a baby elephant anymore, after all. Doing things for myself makes me feel good. And then I get to make the sandwich just the way I like it," he thought. Tony tried what Sally had just shown him. "Not a bad-looking sandwich," he said when he was done. He took a bite. "Tastes pretty good, too!"

While they ate, they all played a guessing game. Outside the volcano had quieted down. It was starting to get dark. After they ate, they all went out to watch the sunset turn purple, pink, and gold behind the volcano. Tony, Sally, and Smiley prepared their beds inside the cave and then snuggled down for the night. In the morning, they would see their Mom. That thought made Tony and Sally feel warm inside. It seemed like they could feel their Mom's love in their hearts, even though she wasn't right there. Tony thought, "I can hardly wait to tell Mom and the tribe about this funny little monkey we've met." With that thought he drifted off to sleep. The others were already dreaming of tomorrow.

CHAPTER 14

Spunky

MITCH BARIS, CARLA GARRITY,
AND KAREN BREUNIG

*This story is written for children with a parent ex-
periencing a substance-abuse problem, but it also has
relevance for any situation in which a parent is self-
absorbed and unable to stay focused on his or her
caretaker role. Embedded in the story are elements to
help the child cope, such as finding alternative adult
role models, helping those less fortunate as a healing
mechanism, and preserving hope for the future, once
emancipated.*

The cottonwoods had turned to gold, the air was crisp,
the circus had come to Springfield again. Spunky sat high
in the stands under the big top watching the circus parade. First the ringmaster, next the procession of animals—the big growling cats and the elephants lumbering
in single file, each holding in its trunk the tail of the animal in front. Next came the jugglers and Juneau the

clown, honking his horn, waving to the crowd of excited onlookers. Then came the acrobats, the trapeze artists, and the great Madame Currigan, the daredevil of the high wire. Then came the performing seals, barking, tossing beach balls, and clapping their fins together. Around and around the rings, all the acts circled and exited through a tiny door at the rear of the circus as the lights and the music and the excitement all faded.

Late that night back in his trailer after the show was over, Spunky sat gazing out across the performers' trailers and the animals' cages. He picked up table scraps from his dinner. He left the trailer he shared with his mother, known to the crowd as Madame Currigan, and headed out for the cages. Sleeper, the seal, muttered little low barking noises as Spunky approached him. Spunky shared his special snack with Sleeper and petted him gently. Sleeper had come to rely on Spunky's "goodnight" visit. Sometimes during the day they would play together with water hoses and inflatable pools. "Here's some dinner," Spunky whispered in the dark. "Goodnight, Sleeper." They visited together, Spunky and Sleeper, a while longer and then Spunky went back to bed at his house at the trailer across the yard.

The next morning, Spunky got up and went to school. There were six students in his elementary school. They were children of all different grades who were taught all together. They had a special tutor who traveled with the circus to teach them. Their tutor was a performer, too, a juggler. Spunky learned some math and he did some reading and went to recess, just like kids in regular schools. Spunky wished he could make more friends. If only he could go to the same school every day, as other kids did. But the circus always traveled—the fall in wheat country, the winter near the orange groves, spring in rolling wooded hill country, and summer where the corn grows tall. Every season, every year, year after year, the circus kept traveling. When the circus travels, the performers' trailers, the animals' cages, the big top, and all the equipment are loaded into freight cars and travel down the tracks to the outskirts of the next town, only to set up again, perform some weeks, load up, and move on. At night from the train windows, Spunky would look at the lights of the houses, knowing a family lived in the yellow glow of the light shining through the windows, families where kids went to the same school all year long, built lasting friendships with classes full of kids their own age, and visited their friends and relatives for holidays.

By lunch time, school was out for the day. Spunky went to visit his friend Juneau, the clown. Juneau had no clown makeup on because it was daytime, and he looked like any other friendly, somewhat graying grownup. Juneau spoke softly to Spunky. They nibbled some lunch and they tossed the ball together today as they had so many days before, but today Juneau had a message for Spunky, one that he knew would make Spunky sad.

"Spunky," Juneau said, "I'll be staying here in Springfield. I told you one day that I would leave the circus and get a permanent home of my own to stay in. I won't be traveling with the circus anymore."

Spunky struggled to see Juneau's face through the tears in his eyes.

Juneau went on. "The hardest part of leaving the circus for me, Spunky, is missing our lunches together, tossing the ball, and being able to be with you as you grow up. Remember, every fall when the circus comes to Springfield, you'll be able to visit with me again. I'll always be here when you get here."

"But what will the circus do without you, Juneau? You're the best clown. There'll never be another clown as funny as you."

"There will be, Spunky," assured Juneau. Spunky was sad.

As the sun began to set, everybody in the circus was getting ready for the arrival of the audience and the beginning of the circus performance. When evening fell, it was time for the acts in the big top to get under way. Spunky took his seat high in the stands, in the dark, looking down on the spotlighted, glittering arena. The show was about to begin.

First leading the circus parade was the ringmaster. He was proud and arrogant, playing to the excited crowd of moms and dads and kids. Next there were the clowns, with their painted smiles and malfitting, colorful clothing and fuzzy wigs. Spunky could spot Juneau among the other clowns by the squirting flower in his jacket pocket. Next came the circus animals, the performing seals clapping their front fins and balancing beach balls on their noses. Then came the elephants in a line, each one's trunk holding the tail of the animal in front, the show horses with their glittery bridles and saddles, ridden by pretty circus acrobats. Then, finally, came Madame Currigan, the graceful, sequined, death-defying act of the high wire. She was in purple tights with billowing chiffon flowing behind each of her movements. She glowed to the crowd, exuding confidence, charm, and beauty. Once again, like so many times before, all the circus performers paraded around and around the arena and finally exited through a little door at the rear where the color and the excitement faded with the lights and the music. The show was about to begin.

The clowns and the seals and the animals and acrobats all performed as the show got under way. After a while, Juneau came to take a seat next to Spunky, as he did every evening in time for Madame Currigan's daring high-wire act. The drums rolled, the ringmaster announced her entry into the main arena, and onto the arena floated Madame Currigan. The drum rolled as she climbed the taut cable into the height of the big top. The audience sat in silent awe and wonder as she first walked and then tumbled and danced in the spotlight in a world seemingly without gravity. The ground seemed not to exist in the darkness far below.

This is the time when Spunky looked away. The audience was hushed, the drums were rolling, and while Spunky couldn't keep his focus on Madame Currigan's death-defying performance, he knew what she was doing by the drum rolls, the gasps of the crowd, the play of the spotlight in the arena. Most important, Spunky knew by the expressions on Juneau's face. Through the painted smile, Spunky could see the look of fear and concern in Juneau's eyes during Madame Currigan's daring routine high above the arena, until at last Juneau's look of concern turned to relief as the music resolved and the crowd roared their approval.

This is the time when Spunky looked away. The audience was hushed, the drums were rolling, and while Spunky couldn't keep his focus on Madame Currigan's death-defying performance, he knew what she was doing by the drum rolls, the gasps of the crowd, the play of the spotlight in the arena.

Spunky wished his Mom, Madame Currigan, would be more like other moms and stay home with him to take care of him. But Spunky knew his Mom needed to perform to the crowd. The crowd always demanded more and more difficult and daring acts as the years went by. Sometimes she would perform without a safety net below. Madame Currigan was a crowd-pleaser, and as much as Spunky wished for it to be different, he knew who his Mom was and that he could not change what she would do with her own life.

And then finally, one day, what Spunky feared the most happened. It was near the end of the high-wire performance. The crowd was hushed, the drums were rolling, and the spotlight was dancing, but Juneau's concerned expression turned to horror and shock, and finally he had to look away himself. The crowd gasped. The great Madame Currigan had fallen from the high wire with no safety net to stop her. Spunky was too frozen with fear to move. He felt his anger, the tears, and sadness all overcome him at once. After the commotion on the arena floor far below was over, Spunky saw Madame Currigan wave to the crowd as she was carried off on a stretcher by ambulance attendants. The crowd roared their approval in support of her courage and their love of her. She hadn't died, Spunky was relieved, but she had broken her leg badly.

Through the next weeks of her recovery, his Mom stayed home with Spunky. She helped him more with his homework, and they took care of their trailer/house together. Spunky took care of her, too. He helped her to walk and to strengthen the muscles she needed to get back her strength and her movement. He brought her things, and he helped her with her rehabilitation exercises. During this time she, too, felt closer to Spunky and relieved that she no longer had to take those risks on the high wire. She, too, agreed that one day soon she would leave the circus, and until she did that, she decided to change to a different circus job that wouldn't require her to take such serious risks. She knew how important she was to Spunky, just as he was to her. As weeks went by and the circus traveled around, Spunky lived in the hope that they could settle in Springfield, near his friend Juneau.

By the time the circus reached Oakville, two towns before Springfield, Madame Currigan's leg had almost fully healed. One night in their trailer, Spunky returned after feeding and visiting Sleeper, the seal. His mom was visiting with her friends—the ringmaster, the animal trainers, and some of the other acrobats. They asked her when she would once again be ready to climb high onto the wire at the top of the big top. To Spunky's relief, she said that she'd decided not to perform anymore. But then her friends reminded her what it felt like to be so appreciated by the crowd. They all told her how they admired her, how they were dazzled by her, and how the crowd adored her and how she made the circus so special with her daring act.

When the circus finally arrived at Springfield, rather than getting off the circuit as Spunky hoped, Madame Currigan decided she would once again resume her act on the high wire. At least Spunky had Juneau there beside him to watch as Madame Currigan again climbed to the heights of the big top. Spunky once more watched the concern in Juneau's face turn to relief. But Juneau no longer had a painted smile. He had a kind, friendly, somewhat wrinkled face and gray hair. Spunky appreciated that it was easier to read Juneau's expressions without the painted smile.

Madame Currigan played to the crowd and their applause. They adored her. She once again resumed traveling with the circus, despite her promises that she would stop. At least Spunky still had Sleeper. Spunky and Juneau agreed that as Spunky continued to travel with the circus, they would write letters, send birthday presents, and visit each year when the cottonwoods turned to gold and the circus played in Springfield, until Spunky grew up.

CHAPTER 15

Nearly Perfect Paradise

MITCH BARIS

Some children experience violence of frightening proportions before the separation of their parents or during the separation and divorce process. The trauma is often overwhelming and long-lasting. Recovery can be slow and the earlier experience of the trauma retriggered by similar events. Recovering hope for a happier and safer future is the theme of "Nearly Perfect Paradise."

Meilo was a little boy who lived with his mother, his father, and his younger sister, Yana, in a small village on an almost perfect South Sea island. Meilo lived in a thatched-roof house, made mostly of bamboo. He slept on a grass mat on a bamboo platform over a dirt floor under a mosquito net. The house had bamboo walls on three sides and was open to the air on the fourth side, where the roof extended far out to keep the occasional rain from coming in, while allowing the smoke from cooking fires to escape. The family didn't need walls at all, because the temperature was just right for living outdoors nearly all day, every day of the year. The sun shone all day most days, except in the short rainy season, when it shone only part of the day. Brightly colored birds flew through the forest treetops by day, while iridescent tropical fishes swam in the shallows of the nearby sea. The villagers made their living by fishing and gathering fruits and growing rice, and raising their own pigs and chickens. Most evenings, cooling breezes would blow through the gently swaying coconut trees on the edge of the nearby tropical forest. The villagers wove beautiful dyed fabrics for clothing and for decoration. Meilo and his family and all the villagers loved their way of life on their most generous and bountiful island home.

The only problem with life on their island was that every few years—and no one ever knew when—violent tropical cyclones would pound their island paradise, causing sometimes great destruction. Meilo heard about strong storms of the past from the village elders. The grandpas and grandmas would tell of their violence and destructiveness. Such a storm had never occurred in Meilo's lifetime, and he hoped it never would. Since there was nothing much that he could do about it anyway, Meilo didn't spend too much time worrying or thinking about it. He knew that if such a storm were to come in his lifetime, he would deal with it as he needed to.

Then one day the horrible happened. It started in the early evening, when the clouds at sunset began to wind around the sky in giant swirls from the horizon—from the sky to the sea and directly overhead. The usual pinks and pastels of the sky turned dark blue and gray and silver and black. Bolts of lightning jumped across the sky and from sky to sea, and rumbles of distant thunder welled up to crashing and deafening roars. As the last daylight faded into black, the land and the sea and the sky began to swirl together, whipped by the strengthening wind. Now the lightning and thunder quieted, but the howling of the wind began to crescendo into screams.

Meilo and his family left the coast as the tides began to chew and then to swallow the white, smooth sands of their beach. The family moved inland to higher ground, to a cave where the other villagers were also arriving with their families and the few things that mattered the most, which they carried with them. In the light of a lantern, the villagers spent the night listening to the lashing and howling wind and hearing the occasional snapping of tree boughs in the jungle outside. After lying awake for hours, Meilo finally fell asleep.

The next morning the villagers awoke in the cave to the sound of silence. The winds had died down, and the cyclone had passed over the island and moved out to sea. It was time to emerge from the cave and inspect the damage the storm left in its wake.

Meilo and his family and the other villagers left the cave together. As they stepped out, each of them fell silent in awe at the power of the cyclone. Right outside the cave where the jungle had been were tangled tree limbs and piles of leaves and green foliage everywhere. Only a few trees were left standing in what had been the jungle.

There were no vines left hanging, and no bird was singing or even visible. The family scrambled down what used to be a path that led to the beach and to the village. Slowly the villagers made their way over the rubble, pushing it aside and trying to rebuild a path for the others behind them to follow. When they approached the village site, more destruction awaited them. Not a house was left standing. Not a boat was left on the beach. All had been carried away by the surf or pounded into debris on the shore. Meilo was frightened. Would his life ever be the same again?

The first year the villagers were helped by international organizations, who supplied tents and tools and food and water and medicine. They were brought in from nearby islands and from distant mainlands. It was wonderful to know that strangers, people he had never met, could care enough to help the islanders. Meilo wondered if his home would be lived in again, or if he could ever feel safe again after such a display of violence and destruction. But he couldn't take too much time to think about it because it was time to rebuild. The villagers, with help from outsiders, rebuilt each house on the site where it had stood. Some were identical to what they had been before, and some were changed—improved or rebuilt bigger and stronger.

Within weeks, the jungle showed signs of growing back. The piles of leaves provided fertilizer for new plants to take root. Within months, the village houses, the boats, and the jungle were back. But the fear didn't go away as quickly. The memories of the sights and sounds of the de-

When they approached the village site, more destruction awaited them. Not a house was left standing. Not a boat was left on the beach.

struction lingered. The memories of the forest destroyed and the village in ruins would come back and frighten Meilo, especially at nighttime when he tried to go to sleep. But Meilo's mother was even more frightened. She knew that if a storm could strike once, it could strike again, maybe even with more fury the next time. Meilo's dad did what he could to reassure her and build back Meilo's mom's trust and confidence, but Meilo's mom decided she would move back to a place where she had once lived on a distant mainland. Meilo's parents were both sad and confused, but together they finally agreed that mom and sister Yana would move away, while Meilo would stay on the island with his dad. They agreed also that Meilo's mom and Yana would return to visit as they could, and that Meilo would make trips to see them as often as possible.

A year went by. The village was rebuilt, and the new growth of the forest was well under way. The villagers went back to fishing, gathering fruit, raising crops and animals, and taking care of themselves. Meilo missed his mom and Yana at some times more than others. He wrote them letters and sent them the dried fragrant petals of a jungle flower he knew they would miss. He always looked forward to their next reunion. However, Meilo's fears and distrust were slow to leave him. He found that talking about his feelings to others helped. His dad and the elders of the village always listened, and at these times they would offer all the reassurances they could about keeping him safe from the violence and destruction, should it occur again. He knew they would do all they could to offer prevention and protection, but there were no guarantees. Meilo knew that to enjoy the almost perfect paradise of living on the island, there would always remain some risk that a violent cyclone could strike again. He could do what he could to get out of its destructive path, as the villagers had before, if he knew it was coming. If it were to strike again, he wondered how many times the villagers could tolerate destruction and rebuild the village. It had happened only a few times throughout history, but if the frequency of the furious storms increased, they would have to rethink whether all of them could live even in a place so nearly perfect so much of the time. Meilo knew he needed to hold on to the hope that it was not likely to strike again.

He heard the elders talking. Some said storms like this one had happened only a few times throughout history. Others said that the storms were coming more frequently. Over time, Meilo's fear diminished but never went away completely. That last bit of fear that he held became part of the wisdom about the ways of the world that Meilo carried with him when he himself became a revered, respected village elder many, many years later.

He relied on his memories of the past to predict and survive future storms. He learned how and when to secure safety.

Suggested Reading

SOME OTHER THERAPEUTIC STORIES FOR
CHILDREN OF FAMILY DISRUPTION

Divorce and Single-Parent Families

Brown, Laurene Krasny & Marc Brown (1986). *Dinosaurs divorce:
A guide for changing families.* New York: Little, Brown.
Tax, Meredith (1981). *Families.* New York: Feminist Press at the
City University of New York.

Geographical Dislocation and Homelessness

Soman, David (1992). *The leaving morning.* New York: Orchard Books.
Testa, Maria (1996). *Someplace to go.* Morton Grove, Ill.: Albert
Whitman.

Domestic Violence and Anger Management

Bernstein, Sharon Chesler (1991). *A family that fights.* Morton
Grove, Ill.: Albert Whitman.
Whitehouse, Elaine & Warwick Pudney (1996). *A volcano in my
tummy: Helping children to handle anger.* P.O. Box 189, Gabriola
Island, B.C. VOR IXO, Canada: New Society Publishers.

Loss and Grief

Brown, Laurene Krasny & Marc Brown (1996). *When dinosaurs die: A guide to understanding death.* New York: Little, Brown.
Palmer, Pat (1994). *"I wish I could hold your hand...": A child's guide to grief and loss.* P.O. Box 1094, San Luis Obispo, Cal. 93401: Impact Publishers.

Separation and Foster Care

Lanners, Karen & Ken Schwartzenberger (Unpublished). *Therapeutic stories for children in foster care.* 508 Higuera St., San Luis Obispo, Cal. 93401. Phone (805) 781-3535: Family Care Network.

Alcoholism

Thomas, Jane Resh (1996). *Daddy doesn't have to be a giant anymore.* New York: Clarion Books.

Sexual Abuse

Davis, Nancy (1988). *Once upon a time...: Therapeutic stories to heal abused children.* Distributed by Self-Esteem Shop, 4607 N. Woodward, Royal Oak, Mich. 48073.
Girard, Linda Walvoord (1984). *My body is private.* Morton Grove, Ill.: Albert Whitman.

OTHER BOOKS FOR COUNSELORS AND PARENTS
ON THERAPEUTIC STORIES

Ayalon, Ofra & Adina Flasher (1993). *Chain reaction: Children and divorce.* Bristol, Pa.: Jessica Kingsley.
Engel, Susan (1995). *The stories children tell: Making sense of the narratives of childhood.* New York: W. H. Freeman.
Gardner, Richard A. (1976). *Psychotherapy with children of divorce.* New York: Jason Aronson.
Lankton, Carol H. & Stephen R. Lankton (1989). *Tales of enchantment: Goal-oriented metaphors for adults and children in therapy.* New York: Brunner/Mazel.

Mills, Joyce & Richard Crowley (1986). *Therapeutic metaphors for children*. New York: Brunner/Mazel.

SOME RESOURCE BOOKS ON CHILDREN IN DIVORCING FAMILIES FOR CONCERNED PARENTS AND MENTAL HEALTH AND LEGAL PROFESSIONALS

Ahrons, Constance (1994). *The good divorce: Keeping your family together when your marriage comes apart*. New York: Harper Perennial.

Cohen, Miriam Galper (1989). *Long distance parenting*. New York: New American Library.

Fouquet, C. Stephen (1996). *Divorced dads*. Minneapolis: Fairview Press.

Garrity, Carla B. & Mitchell A. Baris (1994). *Caught in the middle: Protecting the children of high-conflict divorce*. New York: Lexington Books.

Hodges, William F.(1991). *Interventions for children of divorce: Custody, access, and psychotherapy*, 2d ed. New York: Wiley.

Johnston, Janet R. & Vivienne Roseby (1997). *In the name of the child: A developmental approach to understanding and helping children of high-conflict and violent divorce*. New York: Free Press.

Kalter, Neil (1990). *Growing up with divorce: Helping your child avoid immediate and later emotional problems*. New York: Free Press.

Ricci, Isolina (1997). *Mom's house, dad's house*, 2d ed. New York: Simon & Schuster Fireside Books.

Thomas, Shirley (1995). *Parents are forever*. Langmont, Col.: Springboard.

Wallerstein, Judith S. & Sandra Blakeslee (1989). *Second chances: Men, women & children a decade after divorce*. New York: Ticknor & Fields.

Also of Interest from The Free Press ———

In the Name of the Child: A Developmental Approach to
Understanding and Helping Children of Conflicted and
Violent Divorce

JANET R. JOHNSTON AND VIVIENNE ROSEBY

"A major advance in the understanding and treatment of children
caught in the torment of parental conflict. With clarity and compassion the authors report the impact of witnessing fighting and
violence on emotional, intellectual and moral development, together with new healing methods that they have developed over
many years. Essential reading for judges, family attorneys and all
mental health personnel who work with divorce. This book
changes the field." —Judith M. Wallerstein, Ph.D., author of
Second Chances: Men, Women, and Children a Decade After Divorce

1997 ISBN: 0–684–82771–9

High-Conflict, Violent, and Separating Families: A Group Treatment
Manual for School-Age Children

VIVIENNE ROSEBY AND JANET R. JOHNSTON

"This manual is a rich resource for both novice and experienced
leaders who work with school-age children in groups. Role-play
exercises, drawing, and fantasy imagery activities encourage children to verbalize their feelings, even as they distance themselves
from their parents' conflicts, and develop hope about future rela-
tionships." —Nancy Boyd Webb, DSW, Fordham University Pro-
gram in Child and Adolescent Therapy, and author of *Play Therapy
with Children in Crisis*

1997 ISBN: 0–684–82769–7

Impasses of Divorce: The Dynamics and Resolution of Family Conflict

JANET R. JOHNSTON AND LINDA E. G. CAMPBELL

"Battles over children take place on many fronts, but custody is the critical campaign. . . . Johnston and Campbell have thrown themselves into the midst of such divorce feuds as mediators, clinicians, and investigators. In doing so they have produced a book that is timely, insightful, and practical. . . . The uninitiated will be horrified by the insightful portrayal of the destructive maneuvering carried out in the name of the 'child's best interest.'"
—*Contemporary Psychologist*

1988 ISBN: 0–02–916621–7